Overcoming the Retirement Trap

An 8-Step Financial Freedom Blueprint For Your Journey to Building Wealth, Creating Financial Independence, and Building A Life Beyond Limits

Jeff Kikel

CPTX MEDIA LLC

CPTX Media LLC

Overcoming the Retirement Trap
First Edition

Cover Design: The Cloud Design – 99Designs
Editor: Jeff Kikel
Layout: Jeff Kikel
Publisher: CPTX Media LLC
1320 Arrow Point Dr, Ste 501
Cedar Park, TX 78613

www.CPTXMedia.com

This book is a work of nonfiction based on the author's personal experiences and professional practice. While every effort has been made to ensure the accuracy of the information presented, this book is not intended as a substitute for professional financial advice. Readers should consult with a qualified advisor before making any financial decisions.

Printed in the United States of America.
Print ISBN: 9798288520044

For more information, visit:

www.FreedomDayMethod.com

Contents

Acknowledgements

As I wrap up *Overcoming the Retirement Trap*, I can't help but feel incredibly grateful. This book has been a labor of love—built on years of real conversations, real challenges, and real people chasing freedom. It wouldn't exist without the support, trust, and stories of so many along the way.

First and always, thank you to my wife, business partner, and best friend, Crystal Kikel. Crystal, your belief in our Freedom Day—and in me—never wavered. Through every late night, tough decision, and big dream, you've been my rock. You've lived this journey with me, and your encouragement made it possible to put these ideas on paper. I couldn't have done this without you—and honestly, I wouldn't have wanted to.

To everyone who shared their Freedom Story in this book—thank you. You're the heart of it all. Your courage to step into the unknown and create a new kind of retirement is what makes these pages come alive. Your stories show what's possible when you stop following the traditional script and start writing your own.

To the clients I've worked with over the past 30 years: thank you for trusting me. You let me into your lives, your finances, and your dreams. That's not something I take lightly. It's been the greatest honor of my professional life to walk alongside you.

To the Cubicle Warriors out there grinding away at jobs they've outgrown, and the small business owners burning the candle at both ends—this book is for you. If you're dreaming of a Freedom Day but don't know where to start, I hope this gives you the tools and the nudge to take that first step.

And finally, to my friends, family, mentors, and everyone who's ever encouraged me to keep going—thank you. Your support, feedback, and belief in this mission made all the difference.

At the end of the day, this book isn't just about money. It's about reclaiming your time, your choices, and your life. Here's to building a future that's not just financially secure—but deeply fulfilling.

Thank you for being part of this journey.

– Jeff

Your Free Bonus Resources

Before You Dive In... Get Access to Your Exclusive Retirement Toolkit

As a reader of *Overcoming the Retirement Trap*, you now have **free access** to a complete library of tools and resources designed to help you plan your own Freedom Day.

These are the exact worksheets, calculators, and strategy templates I use with clients every day—and they're all waiting for you.

When you visit
www.freedomdaymethod.com
or scan the QR code below, you'll unlock:

Freedom Day Worksheets – Clarify your vision, track progress, and take control of your plan
Income Planning Spreadsheets – Easy-to-use tools to map out your retirement income strategy
Client Freedom Day Stories – Real-life examples of how others escaped the trap and built a life of purpose
Expert Articles & Blog Posts – Fresh insights and ideas to help you stay on track
Bonus Content & Downloads – Updated tools, printable resources, and insider strategies

This isn't just a book—it's a blueprint. And these free tools are how you bring that blueprint to life.

Visit **www.freedomdaymethod.com** to get started now.

Because retirement isn't the end. It's your beginning.

Scan Here

Chapter One

Introduction

The World Is But A Canvas of Our Imagination. - Henry David Thoreau

Welcome to "Overcoming the Retirement Trap." This book is going to flip everything you think you know about retirement on its head.

I'm not talking about the old-school plan. You know the one. Work for 40 years, save every penny, then maybe—if you're lucky—you can afford to downsize and live on less.

That's garbage.

I'm talking about something way better. I call it your **Freedom Day**. That's the first day you wake up and realize you don't have to go to work unless you want to.

Maybe that sounds impossible right now. Trust me, I get it.

My name is Jeff Kikel. I've spent over three decades learning the ropes of financial planning and entrepreneurship. I've been through the ups, the downs, and all the crazy twists life throws at you.

Here's what I've figured out: The traditional retirement system is broken. It works for maybe 5% of people who either saved a fortune or can live on way less than they made while working.

What about everyone else? They're stuck.

But here's the thing—it's not their fault. They followed the "expert" advice. They did what they were supposed to do. The system failed them, not the other way around.

The Retirement Trap Is Real

Think about this for a second. The "experts" tell you to save 10-15% of your income for 40 years. Put it in a 401k. Hope the stock market doesn't crash right before you retire.

Then, if everything goes perfectly, you might have enough money to live on 70% of your current income.

Wait, what? You work your entire life so you can live on less money?

That's insane.

And here's the kicker: Most people can't even do that. They can't save enough to make the math work. Life gets in the way. Kids need college. The car breaks down. Medical bills pile up.

Even if you do everything right, there's no guarantee it'll work.

I've seen people lose half their retirement savings in market crashes. I've watched others work well into their 70s because they couldn't afford to stop.

The retirement trap is real. And millions of people are stuck in it.

Why This Book Is Different

Most financial books tell you to save more and spend less for 40 years. Then maybe you can retire.

Boring. And unrealistic.

I'm going to show you how to build what I call **cash flow**. That's money coming in whether you work or not.

Big difference.

This isn't about accumulating a giant pile of money and hoping it lasts until you die. It's about creating income streams that pay you for life.

Think about it this way: Would you rather have $1 million in the bank that you're afraid to spend? Or $5,000 a month coming in from investments and businesses for the rest of your life?

I'll take the monthly income every time.

My Personal Wake-Up Call

I learned this lesson the hard way.

In October 2003, I walked into work and found out my job had been eliminated. Eight years with the company. Top performer. Didn't matter.

That's when I realized "job security" is a myth. No matter how good you are, how hard you work, or how long you've been there, someone else controls your paycheck.

And if someone else controls your paycheck, they control your life.

That experience changed everything for me. I decided I was never going to be at the mercy of someone else's decisions again.

It took me years to figure out how to do it right. I made plenty of mistakes along the way. Started businesses that failed. Invested in things I didn't understand. Nearly lost my house at one point.

But I kept learning. Kept adjusting. And eventually, I cracked the code.

Now I'm going to share that code with you.

What You'll Learn

This book breaks down into three key things:

- Building a solid foundation
- Retraining how you think about money
- Developing a cash flow mindset

I'm not just throwing theory at you. This is the exact process I used to reach my own Freedom Day. You'll hear my story and stories from others who've done the same thing.

Stories like Jen Drummond, who almost died in a car crash and decided to climb the Seven Second Summits (the second-highest mountains on all seven continents). She set a Guinness World Record as the first woman to do it.

Or Kim Daly, who thought she wanted to be a doctor but ended up becoming a hugely successful franchise consultant, helping others build businesses using proven systems.

Or Scott Jelinek, who lost 55 properties in the 2008 financial crisis but came back stronger with a completely different approach to real estate investing.

These aren't superhuman people. They're regular folks who refused to accept the conventional path to retirement.

The Best Part

You can start with very little money.

Your background doesn't matter. Your education doesn't matter. Where you come from doesn't matter.

What matters is your desire to change and your willingness to take action.

We live in the most opportunity-rich time in human history. You can learn almost anything for free online. You can start a business with a laptop and an internet connection. You can invest in real estate without owning property.

The tools are there. The opportunities are there.

The only question is: Are you ready to use them?

Your Journey Starts Now

Before we begin, check out our companion website: **www.freedomdaymethod.com**.

You'll find tools, calculators, and videos that go with what you're reading here. Think of it as your support system.

I'm excited to share this with you. Even more excited to hear about your success.

This isn't about getting rich quick. It's about building something sustainable that gives you choices. It's about creating a life where work is optional, not mandatory.

So let's get started. Time to break free from the retirement trap and build a life without limits.

Welcome aboard.

Chapter Two

A Journey Of A Thousand Miles Begins with One Step...

Formal Education Will Make You A Living, Self Education Will Make You A Fortune. -Jim Rohn

I'm going to let you in on a secret.

The entire financial industry has been lying to you. Not on purpose, maybe. But lying all the same.

For almost 30 years, I was part of that industry. I helped people plan for retirement using the same broken system everyone else uses. Save 10-15% of your income. Put it in a 401k. Cross your fingers and hope it works out.

Then about 10 years ago, everything changed for me.

I started seeing two totally different groups of clients walk into my office. And it completely blew my mind.

The Two Groups That Changed Everything

The first group were millennials and Gen Z'ers. They'd read "The 4-Hour Work Week" by Tim Ferriss. They wanted to live life on their terms right now. Travel the world. Work from anywhere. Take "mini-retirements" instead of waiting until they're 65.

These people weren't interested in the traditional 40-year grind. They wanted freedom now, not someday.

The second group? My older clients who felt completely hopeless.

These people had done everything right. They followed every piece of advice the financial industry gave them. Worked 40 years. Saved 10-15% of their income. Put it all in 401ks and IRAs.

And they still couldn't retire.

They'd lived through the dot-com crash of 2000-2003. The Great Recession of 2008-2010. The "lost decade" where their retirement accounts went nowhere.

Many had given up completely. They figured they'd work until they died. Some were talking about downsizing their homes, taking one cruise a year, and wearing black socks with sandals for the rest of their lives.

It was depressing as hell.

The Meeting That Changed Everything

Then I met "Frank."

Frank thought he was stuck in that second group. When he walked into my office, he looked defeated. Said he'd never be able to retire. Figured he'd be working until the day he died.

But when I looked at his numbers, I realized something amazing.

Frank actually had enough money coming in from his investments to cover his living expenses. He just didn't know it.

All this time, he'd been getting up every morning, driving to work, and putting in his eight hours. Not because he had to. But because he thought he had to.

I told Frank he'd already reached "Freedom Day." He had a work-optional lifestyle. He could quit his job tomorrow if he wanted to.

The look on his face was priceless. First confusion. Then a slow smile. Then pure joy.

That's when it hit me. The problem wasn't the money. The problem was how we think about retirement.

Here's What They Don't Tell You

Financial companies train people like me. Their goal? Get you to hand over your money so they can manage it. The more money they control, the more money they make.

I don't blame them. It's their business.

But here's the dirty secret: Their business isn't helping you reach Freedom Day. Their business is collecting assets. They get paid whether your money grows or not.

Think about it. When you meet with a financial advisor, what's the first thing they ask? "How much money do you have to invest?"

They're not asking about your dreams. Your goals. What you actually want your life to look like.

They want to know how much money they can manage for you.

That's backwards.

The entire industry is focused on gathering assets, not helping you create the life you want.

The Real Problem with Traditional Retirement

The old retirement model assumes you'll work for 40 years, save a percentage of your income, then live on less money than you made while working.

But look around. How's that working out?

I've seen people with $2 million in their 401k who are terrified to spend any of it. They're still living like they're broke because they're afraid the money will run out.

I've seen others who saved diligently for decades, only to watch half their retirement disappear in a market crash right before they planned to quit.

The problem is simple: You can't control the stock market. You can't control inflation. You can't control whether your company pension will still exist when you're ready to collect it.

But you can control your income streams.

The Real Game Changer

This book flips the script completely.

We're not focused on accumulating a giant pile of money that might disappear. We're focused on building **cash flow**.

What's cash flow? Money that shows up in your account whether you work or not.

Think rental income from properties. Dividend payments from stocks. Royalties from a book you wrote. Profits from a business that runs without you.

Here's a simple example. Let's say you need $5,000 a month to live comfortably.

The traditional approach says save up $1.5 million, then withdraw 4% per year and hope it lasts until you die.

The Freedom Day approach says build income streams that pay you $6,250 per month (125% of what you need) and never worry about running out of money.

Big difference.

One approach depends on a pile of money that can disappear in a market crash. The other depends on income that keeps flowing no matter what the stock market does.

Which sounds better to you?

Why Most People Never Escape

Most people stay trapped because they're thinking like employees instead of entrepreneurs.

Employees trade time for money. Work 40 hours, get paid for 40 hours. Don't work, don't get paid. It's a direct exchange.

Entrepreneurs build systems that make money without them. They create value once and get paid for it over and over again.

The shift from employee thinking to entrepreneur thinking is the key to everything. That's why we start with a side hustle in this system. Not just for the extra money. To rewire your brain.

Once you start thinking like an entrepreneur, everything changes.

Instead of asking "How can I save more money?" you ask "How can I create more income?"

Instead of cutting out your daily coffee to save $3, you figure out how to make an extra $100 this week.

Completely different mindset. Completely different results.

Why This Actually Works

I've lived this process. Made every mistake in the book. Lost almost everything at one point.

But I figured it out. And now I'm going to save you years of trial and error.

You'll hear stories throughout this book from my Freedom Nation Podcast guests. Regular people who broke free from the 40-year work plan and created their own Freedom Days.

People like Dayana Aleksandrova. She grew up in Bulgaria after the fall of the Soviet Union. Came to America for college but had trouble finding a job because of her foreign passport.

So she decided to chase her dream of becoming a travel blogger. Went to Bali with big plans and quickly realized she needed money to survive anywhere.

She started doing freelance writing for small businesses through Up work.com. Built her skills while living in a tree house at a resort in the Dominican Republic.

Today? She runs two six-figure businesses from anywhere in the world. Lives where she wants, when she wants. Last time I talked to her, she was in southern Spain planning a trip to Malaga for her boyfriend's birthday.

She embodies my favorite quote from Richard Branson: "Screw It, Let's Do It!"

Or take Jim Cathcart. Started as a government clerk at a housing authority in Little Rock, Arkansas, in the 1960s.

One day he heard Earl Nightingale on the radio say: "If you spend an extra hour each day of study in your chosen field, you will be a national expert in that field in five years or less."

Jim took that advice and ran with it. Dedicated an hour a day for five years to learning about success and personal development.

He became one of the world's most sought-after speakers and authors. Written over 20 books. Spoken in over 50 countries. All because he invested one hour a day in himself.

These aren't special people with superhuman abilities. They're regular folks who decided to think differently about work and money.

The Truth About Getting Started

You can start this with very little money.

Your education doesn't matter. Your background doesn't matter.

I know people who've built million-dollar businesses without college degrees. I know college professors who are broke.

Success isn't about what you know when you start. It's about what you're willing to learn and how fast you take action.

The beauty of our world today is that you can learn almost anything for free. YouTube, podcasts, blogs, online courses. The information is out there.

What's missing isn't the knowledge. It's the system to put it all together.

That's what this book gives you.

Your Next Move

Most people read books like this and do nothing. They get excited for a week, then go back to their old habits.

Don't be most people.

The difference between dreamers and achievers is simple: Achievers take the first step.

Your Freedom Day is waiting. It could be tomorrow or 10 years from now. But it's entirely within your control.

Check out our companion website at **www.freedomdaymethod.com**. Download the tools and calculators. Start building your blueprint.

The only question is: How fast do you want to get there?

Let's make it happen.

Chapter Three

And In The Beginning

Picture this.

You wake up tomorrow morning. No alarm clock. You stretch, look out the window, and realize something incredible.

You don't have to go to work today.

Not because you're sick. Not because it's Saturday. But because you have enough money coming in from other sources that work has become optional.

That feeling? That's your Freedom Day.

It's the day your life completely changes. The day you stop being a slave to a paycheck and start living on your own terms.

For me, that day was June 25th, 2022.

My Freedom Day Realization

I was sitting in a local brew pub in Cedar Park, Texas, having what I thought was a casual meeting with my business partner.

Then he dropped a bomb on me.

He wanted to buy me out of our financial planning firm. Said he wanted to take the company in a different direction. A direction that didn't include me.

My first reaction? Pure shock.

I'd spent years building this business. It was my baby. My identity. The thing that got me up every morning.

But then something weird happened.

As I sat there processing what he'd just said, I realized I wasn't devastated. I was... relieved?

That's when it hit me like a lightning bolt.

I didn't need this business anymore. I didn't need any business. I had enough passive income coming in from investments, real estate, and other ventures to cover my expenses.

I was financially free and didn't even know it.

The Moment Everything Changed

That night when I got home, I grabbed a piece of paper and did the math.

Income from rental properties: $2,200 per month.Investment income: $1,200 per month.Income from my other businesses: $3,200 per mo nth.Potential income from the buyout: $6,000 per month.

Total: $12,600 per month.

My expenses? About $8,000 per month.

Holy crap. I'd done it. I'd reached Freedom Day and didn't even realize it.

I was making $4,600 more per month than I was spending. Even if I never worked another day in my life, I could maintain my lifestyle indefinitely.

For the first time in my adult life, I could wake up and choose what to do with my day. Not because someone was paying me to be there. But because I wanted to be there.

The weight that lifted off my shoulders was incredible.

What Freedom Actually Means

At the end of every episode of my Freedom Nation Podcast, I ask guests the same question: "What's your definition of freedom?"

Most people say some version of: "I want to do what I want, when I want, without worrying about money."

That's exactly right.

But here's what most people don't understand. Freedom isn't just about the money. It's about the choice.

Some of my friends who've reached Freedom Day still work. Not because they have to. Because they want to. They love what they do.

Others have completely walked away from their careers to pursue passions they'd put on hold for decades.

The beautiful thing? Both choices are correct. Because they're choosing.

Why I Hate the Word "Retirement"

Retirement is a broken concept.

It assumes you'll work for 40 years, then suddenly stop and live on less money than you made while working. It's based on an industrial age model where people worked in factories until their bodies wore out.

That's not life. That's just waiting to die.

Freedom Day is different. It's not about age. It's not about stopping work forever. It's about reaching a point where work becomes optional instead of mandatory.

I know people who reached Freedom Day at 35. I know others who are still working toward it at 55. Age doesn't matter. What matters is building enough income streams to support the life you want.

The word "retirement" makes people think small. It makes them focus on downsizing, cutting expenses, and living on less.

The word "freedom" makes people think big. It makes them focus on creating more income, building assets, and living on their own terms.

Completely different mindset. Completely different results.

Real People, Real Freedom Days

Let me tell you about some people who've figured this out.

Jim Cathcart started as a government clerk making barely enough to get by. He heard a radio program that said if you study your field for an extra hour a day, you'd become a national expert in five years.

Jim decided to become an expert in success and personal development. One hour a day for five years.

Today he's written over 20 books, spoken in 50+ countries, and makes more money in a month than he used to make in a year. All because he invested one hour a day in himself.

His Freedom Day? He reached it decades ago. But he still works because he loves what he does.

Then there's Jen Drummond. She was living a comfortable suburban life as a mom and business owner. Then she had a near-death experience in a car crash.

That moment changed everything. She realized she'd been putting her life on hold, waiting for "someday" to pursue her dreams.

So she set a goal to climb the Seven Second Summits—the second-highest mountains on all seven continents. Something no woman had ever done.

She became the first woman to complete the challenge and set a Guinness World Record in the process.

Her message? Stop waiting for someday. Start living now.

Or take Kim Daly. She thought she wanted to be a doctor. Took a telemarketing job to pay the bills before medical school.

That job introduced her to franchising. She discovered she had a natural talent for helping people find the right business opportunities.

Today Kim works as a franchise consultant, helping others build businesses using proven systems. She's financially free and gets to help people create their own Freedom Days.

The Choice Is Yours

Here's what all these people have in common: They refused to accept the conventional path.

They didn't wait until 65 to start living. They brought their Freedom Day closer by thinking differently about work and money.

Some built businesses. Others invested in real estate. Some created multiple income streams from various sources.

The path doesn't matter. What matters is the decision to take control of your financial future instead of hoping things work out.

What Your Freedom Day Looks Like

Take a moment right now and imagine your perfect day after reaching Freedom Day.

Where do you wake up? Who are you with? What do you do with your time?

Maybe you travel the world. Maybe you volunteer for causes you care about. Maybe you start that passion project you've been thinking about for years.

Maybe you keep working because you love your job. But now you're there by choice, not necessity.

The beautiful thing about Freedom Day is that it's completely personal. Your version will be different from mine. And that's exactly how it should be.

Getting Started Right Now

Most people think Freedom Day is some distant dream. Something that might happen someday if they're lucky.

That's wrong.

Freedom Day is a decision. A commitment. A systematic process of building income streams that don't require your physical presence.

In the next chapter, we're going to dive into the specific steps to make this happen. The Freedom Day Method that I've refined over years of trial and error.

But first, I need you to get clear on what you're working toward.

Freedom Day Story – Jim Cathcart

From Government Clerk to Stages Around The World
Jim Cathcart started his career as a government clerk in Little Rock Arkansas. One day while listening to a radio broadcast from Earl Nightengale he heard Nightengale say, "With One Extra Hour Of Study Per Day You Can Become A Recognized Expert In 5 Years". Jim took this to heart and put in several hours of study per day becoming a nationally recognized expert in Personal Development in 3 years and being hired to train sales organizations. That expertise has led to writing over 20 books on multiple subjects, being a highly sought after speaker around the world in over 30 countries, recognized in the Speaker's Hall of Fame, and the only person to Keynote three Toastmaster's national conventions. Jim's story is one of growth that started with consistently building his knowledge and expertise one day at a time. My favorite quote that Jim has shared multiple times with me is "Are You The Person Today That Your Future Self Would Want You To Be?". Check out my interview with Jim at: www.freedomdaymethod.com/videos.

Your Freedom Day Blueprint Starts Here

Grab a notebook. This is going to be your Freedom Day journal. You'll use it throughout this entire process.

Answer these questions honestly:

1. What would your ideal lifestyle look like?Don't think about money for now. Just dream. Where would you live? How would you spend your time? What would make you happiest?

2. If money weren't an issue, what would you do every day?Work? Travel? Create? Help others? There's no wrong answer.

3. What are three things you absolutely must do before you die?These will become part of your motivation system.

4. If you could travel anywhere, what are your top three destinations and why?

Take your time with these. Really think about them. These answers will become the foundation for everything we build together.

Your Freedom Day isn't just a financial goal. It's a complete life transformation.

And it starts right now.

Chapter Four

The Journey Of Transformation

Sometimes it takes getting kicked in the teeth to wake you up.

For me, that kick came during what would be my final performance review as an employee. I'll never forget sitting in that sterile conference room, listening to the president of the company deliver the most brutal evaluation of my career.

"Jeff, you're the worst employee we've ever had. You're too independent. You do things without discussing them with management. You act without asking for permission."

Here's the kicker: I was hired specifically to do all those things.

But in that moment, something clicked. I wasn't devastated. I was relieved. This wasn't my failure. This was my wake-up call.

I was never meant to be someone else's employee.

The Breaking Point

For over 25 years, I'd worked for other people in the financial services industry. Sometimes it was fulfilling. Most of the time, it wasn't.

I'd tried starting businesses seven different times. All of them failed. Why? Because I always had a safety net. When things got tough, I'd quit and run back to my "secure" job.

But that performance review changed everything. Three months later, I walked into that office and quit. No safety net. No backup plan. Just pure determination to never work for anyone else again.

Looking back, it was the scariest and best decision I ever made.

The First Taste of Freedom

The seeds of my transformation actually started a few years earlier with a chance meeting.

I'd always wanted to write a book. For 25 years, I kept saying "someday I'll write a book." But someday never came.

Then I met Dr. Joe Serio at a conference. Joe was a former CIA asset and head of the Moscow office of Kroll International. He'd investigated the Russian Mafia and written several books for police officers and special operations.

Over coffee, I mentioned my dream of writing a book. Joe asked the question that changed everything: "Why haven't you done it?"

I gave him my usual excuses. No time. Need company permission. Don't know where to start.

Joe looked me straight in the eye and asked again: "Why haven't you done it?"

I finally gave him the honest answer: "I guess I've just been lazy."

Joe had a book he wanted to write about his time in Russia. I wanted to write a novel series. We made a deal to push each other to get our books done.

Six months later, we published "Leaving Blue: 50 Lessons on Retiring Well From Law Enforcement."

For the first time in my life, I'd created something valuable that could make money without me trading hours for dollars. It was intoxicating.

The Podcast That Changed My Perspective

To promote the book, I decided to start a podcast. Problem was, I'd never listened to a podcast in my life.

I started researching and stumbled across John Lee Dumas's "Entrepreneur on Fire." John had created the first daily business podcast and had over 3,000 episodes at the time.

I binged the first 80-90 episodes. These weren't stories about superhuman entrepreneurs with trust funds and MBA degrees. These were regular people who'd made the leap from employee to business owner.

The lightbulb went off.

These successful people weren't any different from me. They just took action instead of making excuses.

That quote from Jim Cathcart became my North Star. Every decision I made, I asked myself: How would a successful entrepreneur handle this?

The answer was always the same: Take action. Figure it out as you go. Stop waiting for permission.

The Leap Into the Unknown

After that brutal performance review, I knew I had to make a choice. Stay safe and miserable, or leap into the unknown and bet on myself.

I chose to leap.

I quit my job and simultaneously launched two businesses: a coworking space and a financial planning practice. Talk about jumping in the deep end.

The first 18 months were brutal. There were days we barely had enough money for groceries. I sold everything that wasn't nailed down - woodworking tools, video games, books.

But something amazing happened during that struggle. I learned that you can lose your stuff, but you can't lose your ability to create value.

More importantly, I learned the difference between employee thinking and entrepreneur thinking.

The Core Lessons That Changed Everything

Here's what 25 years as an employee couldn't teach me, but 18 months as an entrepreneur did:

Old Ways Don't Work Anymore

The traditional retirement model is broken. Save a percentage of your income for 40 years and hope it's enough? That's not a plan. That's a prayer.

With today's inflation, look around. How many "retired" people are going back to work because their savings aren't enough? The math doesn't work for most people.

Freedom Engines Are the Answer

I started using the term "Freedom Engines" to describe income sources that don't require your physical presence. These can be active (you trade time for money) or passive (money comes in while you sleep).

The goal is building enough Freedom Engines to cover 125% of your living expenses. At that point, work becomes optional.

Think rental properties, dividend-paying stocks, royalties from books, online courses, licensing deals, or businesses that run without you.

Your Path Will Be Unique

Everyone's journey to Freedom Day looks different. Some people love real estate. Others prefer the stock market. Some build online businesses. Others invest in existing companies.

The method doesn't matter. What matters is getting started and staying consistent.

I come from the investment world and love to write. So I focus on income-producing investment strategies and creating books, courses, and content. That feels natural to me.

But I've also learned about digital marketing, online sales, and real estate. Diversification is key.

Action Beats Perfection Every Time

The biggest difference between dreamers and achievers? Dreamers wait for the perfect plan. Achievers start with an imperfect plan and adjust as they go.

I've met hundreds of people who had the same idea for a business I eventually launched. The difference? I actually did it. They kept planning.

The Mindset Shift That Changes Everything

The transformation from employee to entrepreneur isn't just about starting a business. It's about fundamentally changing how you think about problems.

Employees ask: "How can I save more money?"

Entrepreneurs ask: "How can I create more income?"

Employees think: "I can't afford that."

Entrepreneurs think: "What can I do to afford that?"

It sounds like a small difference. But that mindset shift is the difference between staying trapped and breaking free.

Proof This Works for Regular People

Don't take my word for it. Let me tell you about someone who embodies everything I'm talking about.

Freedom Day Story – Dayana Aleksandrova
Screw it. Let's Do It!

Dayana Aleksandrova's story is an inspiring tale of persistence, adaptation, and success in the face of adversity. Growing up in Bulgaria just after the fall of the Soviet Union, Dayana sought freedom and opportunity, teaching herself English and securing a scholarship to study in the United States. However, what she learned in college would not be what helped her achieve her freedom at an early age.

Due to her foreign passport, she faced challenges securing a job after graduation. She ventured into door-to-door sales and later, inspired by a travel blogger, set off to Bali with hopes of becoming a travel blogger herself.

After reaching Bali, Dayana realized how difficult it was to live anywhere without money or a job. She had two choices at this time: either go home and live with her parents in Bulgaria or find a way to make money remotely. She chose the second and began looking for writing jobs where she could write advertising and blogs for small businesses. She did this through Upwork.com.

This led her to a transformative experience in the Dominican Republic, where she lived in a tree house on a resort and began writing blogs and advertisements for them.

Over time, Dayana built her skills and transitioned into copywriting and marketing consulting, eventually creating two successful six-figure remote businesses. Her journey is a remarkable example of how embracing change, leveraging opportunities, and persistent effort can lead to a fulfilling and independent life.

Today, she lives where she wants, when she wants. When I interviewed her, she lived in southern Spain and was about to head to Malaga for a few weeks for her boyfriend's birthday.

Dayana embodies my favorite quote from Richard Branson "Screw It, Let's Do It!".

Check out my interview with Dayana on our companion site at https://www.FreedomDayMethod.com/videos.

Your Transformation Starts Now

Dayana's story proves this works for anyone willing to take action. She didn't have special skills or a trust fund. She had curiosity, determination, and the willingness to figure things out as she went.

That's all you need too.

The question isn't whether you're smart enough, young enough, or qualified enough. The question is: Are you ready to stop making excuses and start taking action?

Your transformation begins the moment you decide you're done living by someone else's rules.

Chapter Homework

Time to get honest about your own transformation. Grab that notebook and answer these questions:

1. What scares you most about taking a different path than most people?

Most people will think you're crazy for pursuing Freedom Day instead of traditional retirement. That's okay. They're not living your life.

2. Which of the "YaButs" do you struggle with most?

- "I don't have enough money to start"
- "I don't have the right education"
- "I can't balance this with my family"
- "I don't know if I have what it takes"

3. Who in your family and friends will support your decision to pursue Freedom Day?

You need cheerleaders. Identify them early.

4. Who in your family and friends will NOT support your decision? Are you okay with that?

Some people will try to talk you out of this. They mean well, but they're projecting their own fears onto you.

The path to Freedom Day isn't for everyone. But if you've read this far, it might be for you.

Ready to keep going?

Chapter Five

Overcoming the Biggest Hurdles on Your Path to Financial Independence

October 2nd, 2003.

I walked into work like any other Thursday morning. Coffee in hand, ready to tackle another day. I'd been with the company for eight years. Top performer. Worked on high-profile projects. I thought I was bulletproof.

This was after three years of one of the toughest stock markets in over five decades. The dot-com crash had wiped out trillions in wealth. Companies everywhere were cutting costs to survive.

Then my boss called me into his office along with several other colleagues.

"We're eliminating your positions," someone from upper management announced.

Turns out, some executive had decided to cut the highest "cost" employees in our department. Didn't matter that we were the most experienced. Didn't matter that we delivered results. We made too much money, so we had to go.

Just like that. Eight years gone. The "secure" job I'd built my life around? Vanished because of a spreadsheet calculation and market forces completely beyond my control.

Sitting in my car in that parking lot, reality hit me like a freight train. There's no such thing as job security. No matter how good you are, how hard you work, or how long you've been there, someone else controls your paycheck.

And if someone else controls your paycheck, they control your life.

That day taught me something crucial: The biggest hurdles to financial independence aren't external. They're the lies we tell ourselves about security, capability, and what's possible.

The Myth That Almost Destroyed Me

For eight years, I believed in "job security." I thought if I worked hard and stayed loyal, the company would take care of me.

What a joke.

The bean counters looked at spreadsheets and decided I made too much money. My performance didn't matter. My loyalty didn't matter. I was just a number that needed to be cut.

But here's the thing that really messed with my head: This wasn't my first wake-up call. I'd tried starting businesses seven times before. Every single one failed.

Why? Because I never fully committed. I always had that "secure" job to fall back on. When things got tough, I'd quit the business and run back to my corporate safety net.

That safety net was actually a prison. It kept me from ever betting on myself.

The job loss forced me to confront a hard truth: The biggest hurdle to financial independence was my own mindset.

The 10 Hurdles That Keep People Trapped

Over the years, I've seen the same obstacles crush people's dreams over and over again. Here are the big ones, and how I learned to overcome them:

Hurdle 1: Believing in Job Security

This is the big lie that keeps millions of people trapped. There's no such thing as a safe job anymore. Companies will drop you the second it benefits their bottom line.

I learned this the hard way in 2003. But it was the best thing that ever happened to me. It forced me to stop depending on others for my financial security.

Hurdle 2: Not Believing in Yourself

Before my breakthrough, I had seven failed businesses Seven times I convinced myself I wasn't cut out for entrepreneurship. Seven times I was wrong.

The difference the eighth time? I burned the ships. No safety net. No backup plan. When failure wasn't an option, I found a way to succeed.

Hurdle 3: Caring What Others Think

When I finally quit my job to start my own business, my parents thought I'd lost my mind. My work friends couldn't understand why I'd give up a "good job."

You know what? They weren't living my life. I was.

The path to Freedom Day is the road less traveled. Most people won't understand it because most people are content being average.

Hurdle 4: Not Finding Your Tribe

The Freedom Day journey can be lonely. You're not following the traditional path, so you need to find others who are on the same journey.

I started networking like crazy. Ten events per week. Meet two people per event. Schedule one-on-one meetings to build relationships.

Over four years, I met with 2,205 people. That network became my support system, my sounding board, and my source of opportunities.

Hurdle 5: Thinking You Need to Do Everything Yourself

I'm an introvert. Networking terrified me. But I created a system and stuck to it. Half the events were lunches (I had to eat anyway). The others were morning meetings or happy hours.

If an extreme introvert like me can build a network of thousands, anyone can.

Hurdle 6: Staying Flexible While Staying Focused

The path to Freedom Day isn't straight. You'll hit obstacles. You'll need to pivot. The key is staying committed to the destination while being flexible about the route.

I've had to change strategies multiple times. Each setback taught me something valuable. Each adjustment got me closer to my goal.

Hurdle 7: Building Resilience When Things Go Wrong

Every successful entrepreneur has war stories. I almost lost my house. I've seen businesses fail overnight. I've made investments that went to zero.

But here's what I learned: Every failure contains the seeds of the next success. You just have to be willing to learn from it and keep going.

Hurdle 8: Overcoming Fear

Fear is normal. Fear of failure. Fear of success. Fear of what people will think.

I used to let fear paralyze me. Now I use it as fuel. When I'm scared of something, I know it's probably worth doing.

The question isn't whether you'll feel fear. The question is whether you'll let fear stop you.

Hurdle 9: Creating a Solid Plan

Most people fail because they don't have a system. They wing it and hope for the best.

The Freedom Day Method gives you a step-by-step blueprint. Follow the steps in order. Don't skip ahead. Don't try to reinvent the wheel.

Hurdle 10: Continuing to Learn and Grow

The most successful people I know are voracious learners. They read constantly. They invest in themselves. They never stop growing.

Formal education teaches you to be a good employee. Self-education teaches you to be financially free.

Why Community Matters More Than You Think

Here's something most people don't understand: The journey to Freedom Day is as much about who you become as what you achieve.

You need mentors who've done what you want to do. You need peers who are on the same journey. You need people you can mentor who are behind you.

I spend 25% of my community time mentoring others earlier in their journey. Another 25% networking with peers at my level. The final 25% learning from mentors ahead of me.

This isn't just about business. It's about surrounding yourself with people who challenge you to grow.

Proof That Anyone Can Overcome These Hurdles

Let me tell you about someone who faced obstacles that make most people's problems look trivial.

Freedom Day Story – Jenn Drummond

Mastering the Seven Second Summits

Jenn Drummond's journey is a testament to resilience and determination. Once a stay-at-home mom and business owner, Jenn's life took a dramatic turn following a near-fatal car crash in 2018. This incident served as a wake-up call, prompting her to stop putting her life on hold and start living fully.

Jenn embarked on a remarkable adventure, climbing the second-highest mountains on the seven continents, also known as the "Seven Second Summits." Her decision was fueled by her desire to demonstrate to her children, especially her son, that any personal 'Everest' can be conquered.

Jenn successfully achieved this feat, becoming the first woman to do so, and holds a Guinness World Record for her accomplishment. Her experiences have since been transformed into a book and motivational speeches, inspiring others to pursue their dreams and overcome challenges.

Jenn's story is a powerful example of how a life-altering event can lead to extraordinary achievements and personal growth.

You can listen to my full interview with Jenn on our companion site, www.FreedomDayMethod.com/videos.

The Choice Is Yours

Jenn's story proves something important: The biggest hurdles aren't external. They're internal.

She didn't have special mountaineering skills when she started. She didn't have unlimited money. She had something more powerful: The decision to stop making excuses and start taking action.

That's available to you too.

Every hurdle I've mentioned can be overcome. Every obstacle can be navigated. Every fear can be conquered.

But only if you decide to do it.

Your Path Forward

The hurdles are real. I'm not going to sugarcoat that. Building financial independence requires you to think differently, act differently, and persist when things get tough.

But here's what I've learned: The regret of not trying is far worse than the fear of failing.

You can spend the next 10 years making excuses. Or you can spend them building the life you actually want.

The choice is yours.

Chapter Homework

Time to identify your personal hurdles and create a plan to overcome them. For each hurdle below, answer these questions in your notebook:

1. What specific actions can I take to overcome this hurdle?Think practical steps that move you forward, not just positive thinking.

2. Who or what resources can support me in overcoming this hurdle?Identify people, communities, books, or online resources that offer guidance.

3. How will overcoming this hurdle bring me closer to my Freedom Day?Connect each challenge to your bigger goal to stay motivated.

The Hurdles to Analyze:

- Believing in job security
- Not believing in yourself

- Caring what others think
- Not finding your tribe
- Thinking you need perfect conditions
- Being inflexible when plans change
- Giving up when things get hard
- Letting fear paralyze you
- Not having a solid plan
- Stopping learning and growing

Remember: These hurdles stopped me for years. But once I learned to overcome them, everything changed.

Your Freedom Day is on the other side of these obstacles. The question is: How badly do you want it?

Chapter Six

The Secrets to Unlocking Your Freedom Day

I was sitting on my couch at 2 AM, surrounded by bills I couldn't pay.

It was month 14 of my entrepreneurial journey. I'd quit my corporate job with big dreams and unlimited confidence. Two businesses launched simultaneously. A financial planning practice and a coworking space. I was going to conquer the world.

Instead, I was about to lose my house.

The coworking space was bleeding money. The financial planning practice had about 20 clients, but they weren't generating enough revenue to cover my expenses. We'd sold everything that wasn't nailed down - my woodworking tools, video games, collectibles. I was working 80-hour weeks and somehow moving backwards.

That night, staring at those bills, I had a brutal realization: Working harder wasn't the answer. I needed to work smarter.

More importantly, I needed a system.

The Breakdown That Led to the Breakthrough

Up until that point, I was running on pure hustle and hope. No real strategy. No clear priorities. Just throwing everything at the wall and praying something would stick.

I was making every mistake in the entrepreneur playbook:

Chasing every opportunity that came my way. Saying yes to projects that paid little and took forever. Spending money I didn't have on things that didn't matter. Working on urgent tasks instead of important ones.

Most damaging of all: I had no clear picture of what success actually looked like.

I was busy as hell but getting nowhere fast.

That 2 AM moment forced me to step back and ask the hard questions: What was I actually trying to accomplish? Why was I spinning my wheels? How could other people build successful businesses while I was struggling to keep the lights on?

The answer came down to three things I was doing completely wrong.

Secret #1: Master Your Time Before Your Time Masters You

For the first year and a half, I confused being busy with being productive.

I'd work from 6 AM to 10 PM every day. I felt like I was grinding harder than anyone. But at the end of each week, I couldn't point to anything meaningful I'd accomplished.

The problem wasn't the number of hours. It was how I was using them.

I was spending 80% of my time on tasks that generated 20% of my results. Customer service issues. Administrative busy work. Chasing small clients who demanded massive amounts of attention.

Meanwhile, the activities that could actually grow my business - networking, content creation, strategic planning - got squeezed into whatever time was left over.

The Time Audit That Changed Everything

I started tracking how I spent every hour for two weeks. The results were shocking.

Only 12 hours per week were spent on revenue-generating activities. Twelve hours out of 80!

The rest was consumed by what I call "fake work." Tasks that felt important but didn't move the needle. Email. Social media. Reorganizing files. Attending meetings that could have been emails. Networking with the wrong people who had no interest in what I was offering.

I implemented a simple system: The Revenue Hour Rule.

Every day, I had to complete at least one hour of revenue-generating activity before I could do anything else. Sales calls. Content creation. Networking. Building partnerships.

Some days I did more than one hour. But I never did less.

That one change doubled my income in six months.

Time Leverage Changes Everything

Once I mastered my own time, I learned to leverage other people's time.

I started outsourcing everything I wasn't uniquely qualified to do. Virtual assistants handled admin work. Freelancers created content. Automated systems managed routine tasks.

This freed me up to focus on the activities that only I could do. Strategy. Relationship building. High-level decision making.

The goal isn't to work less (though that's a nice side effect). The goal is to make sure every hour you work is moving you closer to Freedom Day.

Secret #2: Your Money Should Work Harder Than You Do

My second major mistake was thinking like an employee about money.

Employees trade time for money. Work 40 hours, get paid for 40 hours. Don't work, don't get paid.

I was running businesses but still thinking like an employee. If I wasn't actively working, money wasn't coming in.

That's backwards.

The Cash Flow Awakening

The breakthrough came when I started studying successful investors and entrepreneurs. I noticed something interesting: They focused on building systems that generated income without their constant involvement.

Robert Kiyosaki calls this the difference between the four quadrants in his Cashflow Quadrant model.

"E" (Employee) - You work for someone else and trade time for money.

"S" (Self-Employed) - You own a job. You're still trading time for money, but you work for yourself. Most small business owners fall into this category. If you stop working, the money stops coming.

"B" (Business Owner) - You own a system that works without you. Other people run the business while you collect the profits.

"I" (Investor) - Your money works for you through investments that generate passive income.

At this point in my journey, I was stuck in the "S" quadrant. I owned my businesses, but they completely depended on me. If I took a vacation, revenue dropped. If I got sick, nothing happened.

I had to shift from being self-employed in the "S" quadrant to building true "B" quadrant businesses and "I" quadrant investments.

I had to shift from trading time for money to building assets that produced cash flow.

Building Your First Freedom Engine

My first real Freedom Engine was the coworking space. Despite nearly bankrupting me at the start, I learned valuable lessons about cash flow businesses.

Once I got the model right, that space generated $4,000-$6,000 per month in profit without requiring my daily involvement. I had a manager who handled the operations. I just collected the checks.

That taught me the power of what I now call "Freedom Engines" - income sources that don't require your physical presence.

Since then, I've built multiple Freedom Engines:

- Rental properties that generate monthly cash flow
- Investment portfolios that pay dividends
- Online courses that sell while I sleep
- Books that earn royalties years after I wrote them
- Licensing deals that pay ongoing fees

The 125% Rule

Here's the magic number: When your Freedom Engines generate 125% of your living expenses, you've reached Freedom Day.

Why 125% instead of 100%? Because life happens. Markets fluctuate. Expenses pop up. That 25% buffer gives you peace of mind and covers inflation.

My current living expenses are about $8,000 per month. So I need $10,000 per month from Freedom Engines to maintain my lifestyle without working.

Once I crossed that threshold, everything changed. Work became a choice, not a necessity.

Secret #3: Intention Turns Dreams into Reality

The third secret took me the longest to understand: Having a systematic approach to turn intentions into daily actions.

For years, I was working hard but without clear execution. I'd set annual goals, then promptly forget about them. I'd have great intentions but no system to make them happen.

That's when I developed what I call the I.D.E.A. method.

The Battle Plan That Changed Everything

Every quarter, I create what I call my "Battle Plan" - a big poster on my office wall with a grid: 8 verticals (my 8 quarterly goals) by 13 horizontals (weeks in the quarter).

I break each quarterly goal into specific weekly steps and write them on Post-It notes. Then I stick them on the grid so I can see exactly what needs to happen each week to hit my quarterly targets.

This isn't just goal-setting. It's goal execution.

Each week, I pull three category goals from my Battle Plan and break them down into daily actions. My "big three" for each day go straight into my calendar.

But here's where most people stop. They plan but don't execute efficiently.

That's where I.D.E.A. comes in.

(I)dentify Everything

Every morning, I identify everything that needs to be done that day. Not just my big three goals, but emails that came in overnight, personal tasks, things that rolled over from yesterday.

I get it all out of my head and onto paper.

(D)elegate What Others Can Do

Next, I review my task list and delegate everything possible. My VA in the Philippines gets tasks in the morning that are often completed before I even get to the office (time zone advantage).

Team members in the States get their assignments immediately. If it can be done by someone else, it gets delegated.

(E)liminate the Unnecessary

This is my favorite step. I look for tasks that can be completely eliminated.

Before using this system, I'd have a full page of tasks daily and only complete about 20% of them. Those incomplete tasks would carry over to the next day, creating an ever-growing pile of stress.

Then I realized something: When I eliminated hundreds of incomplete tasks, no one cared. Nothing bad happened. I'd been creating work that didn't need to exist.

(A)utomate the Repetitive

Finally, I identify tasks that are important but repetitive and find ways to automate them. Follow-up emails, automated payments, recurring reports.

I've recently started using AI tools for research, outlines, and first drafts. This book was primarily created with AI assistance, leaving me to focus on adding the personal stories and insights only I can provide.

Why This System Actually Works

The I.D.E.A. method works because it bridges the gap between intention and execution.

Most people set goals but have no daily system to achieve them. Others get lost in daily tasks without connecting them to bigger objectives.

I.D.E.A. solves both problems. It connects your quarterly goals to daily actions, then helps you execute those actions efficiently.

The result? I'm more effective than I've ever been, with less stress and better results.

Why All Three Secrets Work Together

Here's the thing about these three secrets: They're not separate strategies. They work together as a system.

Time management without money leverage just makes you a more efficient employee.

Money strategies without time management keep you trapped in the hustle.

Clear intention without the other two is just wishful thinking.

But when you master all three, magic happens.

You start making strategic decisions instead of reactive ones. You build assets that compound over time. You work toward a specific destination instead of wandering aimlessly.

Most importantly, you start living intentionally instead of accidentally.

Proof That These Secrets Create Multiple Freedom Engines

Let me share a story about someone who mastered all three secrets to build multiple income streams.

Freedom Day Story – John Crestani Affiliate Marketing Leads to Massive Success and Further Diversification

John Crestani's journey, as shared on the Freedom Nation Podcast, is a remarkable story of ambition, innovation, and success. Crestani's entrepreneurial spirit was evident from his college days when he leveraged opportunities to earn money through innovative means like selling study guides. His foray into marketing and sales led him to a job at a marketing agency, but it was only a short time before he ventured out on his own. Crestani's transition to affiliate marketing was a game-changer, skyrocketing his income and setting the stage for future endeavors.

His success in affiliate marketing inspired him to share his knowledge of starting an online business through information products. This venture continued to thrive, allowing Crestani to diversify into real estate and other investments. His latest project, Advanced Pay, focuses on influencer analytics and marketing to optimize ROI in the influencer space.

Crestani's story is a testament to the power of hard work, strategic thinking, and the willingness to adapt and evolve in the dynamic world of digital marketing.

Check out the Full Interview with John on our companion site: https://www.FreedomDayMethod.com/videos. Even though it does not directly match this chapter I want to include him here. He is a master of creating different sources of income going from affiliate marketing to teaching people how to do affiliate marketing.

The Compound Effect of Small Changes

The beautiful thing about these three secrets is that small improvements compound over time.

Saving one hour a day gives you 365 extra hours per year. That's nine weeks of additional time to work on your Freedom Engines.

Building one new income stream that generates $500 per month adds $6,000 per year to your passive income.

Writing down your goals and reviewing them quarterly dramatically increases your odds of achieving them.

These aren't massive changes. They're small, consistent adjustments that create massive results over time.

Your Implementation Strategy

Most people read about strategies like this and do nothing. They get excited for a week, then go back to their old habits.

Don't be most people.

Pick one secret and focus on it for 30 days. Master it before moving to the next one.

If you're constantly overwhelmed, start with time management. If you're working hard but not building wealth, focus on money strategies. If you're busy but directionless, clarify your intentions first.

The order doesn't matter as much as taking action.

Chapter Homework

Time to audit your current situation and identify which secret needs your immediate attention.

Time Audit: Track how you spend every hour for one week. Categorize each activity as:

- Revenue-generating
- Important but not urgent
- Urgent but not important
- Neither important nor urgent

What percentage of your time is spent in each category?

Money Flow Analysis: List all your current income sources:

- How many require your physical presence?
- How many generate income while you sleep?
- What's your ratio of active vs. passive income?

Intention Clarity Check: Answer these questions:

- What specific lifestyle do you want Freedom Day to provide?
- What would you do with your time if money wasn't a concern?
- How will you know when you've "made it"?
- What metrics will you track to measure progress?

Your Next 30 Days: Based on your audit, choose ONE area to focus on for the next month:

If you chose TIME: Implement the Revenue Hour Rule. One hour of revenue-generating activity before anything else each day.

If you chose MONEY: Identify one potential Freedom Engine you could start building this month. Research it thoroughly.

If you chose INTENTION: Create your Freedom Day vision and write down specific, measurable goals with deadlines.

Remember: These three secrets didn't save my business overnight. But they turned me from a struggling entrepreneur into someone living on their own terms.

They'll do the same for you if you implement them consistently.

Your Freedom Day is waiting. Time to unlock it.

Chapter Seven

What's The Catch? Preparing For The "Suck"

Month 17. I walked through the front door of our house and collapsed onto the couch.

Crystal took one look at my face and knew. The coworking space was hemorrhaging cash. Again. Our second summer in business, and every entrepreneur we counted on had decided to take the season off. No members meant no revenue. But the rent, utilities, internet, and employee paychecks? Those kept coming.

My wealth management practice was growing, but barely generating enough to cover groceries, let alone save the business. I stared at the ceiling, running the numbers for the hundredth time that day. No matter how I sliced it, we were drowning.

"I don't know what to do," I said, my voice barely above a whisper.

Crystal sat down beside me. After seventeen months of watching me pour everything into this dream, seeing me work 80-hour weeks and sacrifice every comfort we'd known, she said the words I'd been dreading:

"We're going to have to close the business."

The silence stretched between us. Everything in my rational mind agreed with her. The smart thing—the logical thing—was to cut our losses, admit defeat, and find a way back to financial stability.

But something deeper was stirring.

The Moment That Changes Everything

I looked at Crystal and shook my head. "I can't."

"Jeff, we're broke. We can't keep—"

"I feel an obligation," I interrupted. "To the people who put their trust in us. Who supported us. Who believed in what we were building."

That's when the real catch of Freedom Day hit me like a freight train.

The catch isn't that the method doesn't work. The catch is that pursuing it will test every fiber of who you are.

Sitting in that living room, facing financial ruin, I had a choice. Take the easy way out, or remember something I'd learned as an infantry soldier: When you're carrying a heavy rucksack on a difficult march, and every muscle is screaming at you to quit, you do one thing.

Put one foot in front of the other. And keep doing that until you reach your destination.

Welcome to "The Suck"

What I didn't know at the time is that month 17 is when most small businesses die. I now call it "The Suck"—that period around 18 months when reality hits hard, the initial excitement has worn off, and the gap between your dreams and your bank account feels insurmountable.

Statistics show that 80% of small businesses fail within the first 18 months. Not because their ideas are bad. Not because they lack skills.

But because they reach The Suck and don't know how to push through.

That night, instead of planning our business funeral, Crystal and I rolled up our sleeves. If we were going to save this thing, we needed to get resourceful fast.

The Infantry Solution

The next morning, I went into full infantry mode:

Renegotiated payments with creditors. I called every vendor and explained our situation honestly. Most were willing to work with us.

Eliminated expensive services. We cut every non-essential expense. If it didn't directly serve our members, it was gone.

Reduced our internet costs. Found a cheaper provider that met our basic needs.

Streamlined staffing. We had to let go of an employee, which hurt, but it was necessary for survival.

Brought Crystal on as manager. She worked for equity instead of salary (and did an incredible job).

Was it comfortable? Hell no. Was it sustainable? Barely. But it got us through The Suck.

We haven't looked back since.

The Real Catch Revealed

So what's the catch with the Freedom Day Method? Here's the brutal truth:

It's not a get-rich-quick scheme. You'll work harder than you've ever worked in your life.

It will test your relationships. Your spouse, family, and friends will question your sanity. Some may not understand why you'd give up "security" for uncertainty.

You'll face moments of absolute terror. Times when quitting seems like the only rational option.

Most people won't make it through The Suck. Around month 18, when the initial excitement wears off and reality sets in, the majority of people quit.

But here's what they don't tell you about that catch: **It's also the greatest filter you'll ever encounter.**

The people who push through The Suck? They develop something that can't be taught in business school: unshakeable resilience. They learn that they're capable of far more than they ever imagined.

Why Traditional Retirement Planning Feels "Safe"

Now I understand why most people stick with the traditional path. It's not because 401(k)s and mutual funds are superior strategies. It's because they never ask you to face The Suck.

With traditional retirement planning, you:

- Show up to work
- Contribute to your 401(k)
- Hope the market performs
- Cross your fingers that you'll have enough at 65

It feels safe because someone else is making the decisions. You're not responsible for the outcome—the market is, your employer is, the government is. Anyone but you.

The Freedom Day path puts you squarely in the driver's seat. That's exhilarating and terrifying in equal measure.

Embracing a Different Strategy

The catch isn't a bug in the Freedom Day Method—it's a feature. Because here's what happens when you push through The Suck:

You develop antifragility. You learn to not just survive crisis, but to grow stronger from it.

You build real skills. Skills that no economic downturn or corporate restructuring can take away from you.

You create multiple income streams. So you're never again dependent on someone else's decision to keep paying you.

You prove to yourself what you're capable of. And that confidence becomes unshakeable.

The Truth About Self-Help Books

Here's another catch: Information alone won't save you during The Suck.

I'd read every business book on the shelf. I had theories, strategies, and frameworks coming out of my ears. But when I was sitting on that couch, facing bankruptcy, none of that mattered.

What mattered was my willingness to act. To make the hard decisions. To keep moving forward when every logical voice in my head was screaming "QUIT!"

Most people who buy self-help books never finish them. Of those who do finish them, most never implement what they've learned. And of those who start implementing, most quit at the first sign of real difficulty.

If you're reading this, you're already ahead of 90% of people. But reading isn't enough. You have to be willing to walk through The Suck.

Building Your Support Network

One thing that became crystal clear during our darkest months: you cannot do this alone.

The traditional career path provides built-in community. Coworkers, office politics, shared experiences. When you strike out on your own, that social structure disappears.

I learned to build my network strategically. Over four years, I attended ten networking events per week, met at least two people at each event, and scheduled one-on-one meetings with them the following week.

2,205 people. That's how many one-on-one meetings I had.

Was it exhausting for an introvert like me? Absolutely. But that network became my lifeline during The Suck. When I needed vendors who would work with payment plans, when I needed referrals, when I just needed someone who understood the entrepreneurial journey—my network was there.

For introverts reading this: I get it. The thought of networking makes you want to hide under your desk. But here's the thing—introverts are actually better at building meaningful professional relationships because we prefer deep, one-on-one connections over superficial group interactions.

You don't need to work the room at cocktail parties. You need to have coffee with people who share your struggles and aspirations.

The Momentum Problem

The hardest part of The Suck isn't the external challenges—it's the internal ones.

For twenty-five years, I'd been conditioned to show up at 9 AM, do my work, and go home at 5 PM. Rinse and repeat. There was a comfort in that monotony, even if it was slowly killing my soul.

When you're building your Freedom Day path, every day is different. Some days you make progress. Some days you feel like you're moving backward. The uncertainty can be paralyzing.

I learned to create my own momentum through what I now call "micro-wins." Every small success—a new client, a problem solved, a creditor who agreed to new terms—became fuel for the next day.

The key is to celebrate progress, not just results. Because during The Suck, results can be scarce. But progress? That's happening every day if you know how to look for it.

Breaking Free from Conventional Thinking

The biggest shift isn't financial—it's psychological.

You have to retrain your brain from employee thinking ("I can't afford that") to entrepreneur thinking ("How can I afford that?").

When we needed to reduce our internet costs, I didn't just accept the first quote I received. I researched alternatives, negotiated with providers, and found creative solutions. That simple mindset shift saved us hundreds of dollars per month.

This applies to everything: finding customers, solving problems, generating income. The question isn't "Can I do this?" The question is "How can I make this work?"

What's Waiting on the Other Side

Here's what nobody tells you about pushing through The Suck: the view from the other side is spectacular.

Yes, the journey is harder than traditional retirement planning. Yes, you'll face moments of doubt and terror. Yes, most people will think you're crazy.

But the people who make it through? They live with a freedom that most people can't even imagine.

They wake up each day knowing they're in control of their time, their income, and their future. They've proven to themselves that they can handle whatever life throws at them. They've built something that can't be taken away by corporate restructuring or economic downturns.

That's worth every moment of The Suck.

Freedom Day Story – Matthew Pollard

Never Stop Learning and Striving

Matthew Pollard's story is a remarkable tale of resilience, learning, and success that perfectly illustrates how to push through The Suck.

A reading disability caused him to have the reading speed of a sixth grader in late high school, where he struggled academically. After graduation, Matthew faced significant challenges in finding a job—the only one he could get at the time was door-to-door sales selling vacuum cleaners.

Not only did Matthew have absolutely no sales experience, but he was also incredibly introverted and struggled to speak to people.

Talk about The Suck. Reading disabilities, introversion, job loss, and being forced into sales—the exact opposite of his natural strengths.

But here's where Matthew's story becomes inspiring: instead of quitting, he turned to YouTube to learn sales and management skills, applying them diligently. This self-education led him to become the number one salesperson in his company, and eventually, he started his own business.

After moving to the United States to be with his future wife, Matthew began a relentless journey that led to him becoming one of the most sought-after speakers worldwide and also to becoming the best-selling author of "The Introverts Edge" and "The Introvert's Edge to Networking," where Matthew shares his techniques for helping introverts become successful in business and life.

Matthew's story highlights the importance of self-learning, developing systems, and perseverance. He created multimillion-dollar success stories, emphasizing that introverts can excel in sales and networking with the right approach.

His journey from struggling with essential reading to becoming a successful entrepreneur and coach is genuinely inspiring. Most

importantly, it shows what's possible when you refuse to let The Suck defeat you.
Check out my interview with Matthew at our companion site: https://www.FreedomDayMethod.com/videos

Preparing for What's Ahead

As you start this path, understand that The Suck is coming. It's not a matter of if—it's when.

Surround yourself with people who support your vision. This might not be your current friends and family. The Freedom Day path isn't for everyone, and not everyone will understand why you'd sacrifice current comfort for future freedom.

Find others on similar journeys. Whether it's real estate investors, entrepreneurs, or other people building passive income streams, connect with people who get it.

Build your financial cushion before you leap. Learn from my mistakes. Having some runway makes The Suck more manageable.

Develop your mental resilience. Read about other entrepreneurs who've faced adversity. Study their strategies. Understand that what you're going through is normal and temporary.

Conclusion: Owning the Journey

As we close Chapter Seven, remember that the "catch" of the Freedom Day Method isn't a reason to avoid it—it's a reason to respect it.

This journey will ask more of you than any corporate job ever will. It will test your resolve, challenge your assumptions, and force you to grow in ways you never expected.

But for those who persist through The Suck, who keep putting one foot in front of the other when everything seems hopeless, the rewards are extraordinary.

The question isn't whether you'll face The Suck. The question is: when you do, will you have the courage to keep moving forward?

That's the real catch. And it's also the real opportunity.

Chapter Homework

Objective: Prepare mentally and practically for The Suck by identifying your potential breaking points and building your support system.

Step 1: Identify Your Breaking Point

Write honestly about:

1. What scares you most about taking a different path than most people?
2. What would be your likely breaking point? (Financial? Social pressure? Time stress?)
3. What would you tell yourself in month 17 when everything looks hopeless?

Step 2: Build Your Early Warning System

1. What are three early signs that you're approaching burnout or your breaking point?
2. Who in your life would give you honest feedback about your mental state?
3. What are three specific actions you could take to reset when things get tough?

Step 3: Create Your Support Network Plan

1. List 5 people in your current network who would support your Freedom Day journey

2. Identify 3 types of people you need to meet (mentors, peers, potential customers)

3. Research 3 local or online communities related to your chosen path

Step 4: Prepare Your "One Foot Forward" Strategy

Drawing from the military mindset that saved Jeff's business:

1. What's your version of "one foot in front of the other"?

2. What daily or weekly action could you commit to, even when motivation is gone?

3. How will you measure progress when results aren't visible yet?

Remember: The goal isn't to avoid The Suck—it's to be prepared when it arrives. Every entrepreneur faces it. The successful ones are simply the ones who keep moving forward.

Chapter Eight

The Freedom Day Method – Your Blueprint to Financial Independence

Sometimes the worst things that happen to us can lead to the best breakthroughs.

March 2020. The world shut down.

Crystal and I got up every morning during the pandemic lockdowns and went to work. While most businesses in our area were forced to close their doors, we got lucky. We manage clients' mail as an additional cash flow source we'd been building for years. That made us "essential."

So while everyone else was home in their pajamas doing Zoom calls, we were still going to the office every day.

But here's the crazy part.

I went from working 80 hours a week to working around 35 hours a week. And we had the best year we'd ever had in business.

The Lightbulb Moment That Changed Everything

During those quiet months, something clicked for me.

I'd already been using the term "Freedom Day" with my financial planning clients. But I realized I needed to create an actual system - a step-by-step method that would explain how to get there.

More importantly, I realized I couldn't go back to working 80-hour weeks when things returned to "normal."

That's when I started focusing on reaching my own Freedom Day.

I began systematically working through what would become the 8-step Freedom Day Method:

- Focusing on our budget and eliminating debt
- Adjusting my businesses from S-style (self-employed) to B-style (true businesses)
- Launching other sources of passive income to grow our monthly income

This all led up to the sale of my business and my actual Freedom Day.

But here's what I learned during those pandemic months: Working harder doesn't equal working smarter.

Why Most People Never Reach Financial Freedom

Before the pandemic forced me to slow down, I was like most entrepreneurs and ambitious employees. I thought success meant cramming more into every day.

More meetings. More projects. More hustle.

I was dead wrong.

The pandemic taught me that when you focus on the right things - the things that actually move the needle - you can work half the hours and get twice the results.

That's exactly what the Freedom Day Method does. It forces you to focus only on what matters.

The Birth of a System

During those 35-hour work weeks, I had time to think. Time to analyze what was actually working in my business versus what was just keeping me busy.

I started documenting everything:

- Which activities generated real income
- Which ones were just "fake work"
- How to build systems that worked without me
- The exact order you need to tackle things for maximum impact

What emerged was an 8-step blueprint that could take anyone from their current situation to complete financial independence.

I tested it on myself first. It worked.

Then I started sharing it with clients. It worked for them too.

The 8 Steps That Change Everything

Here's the framework that came out of those pandemic months:

Step 1: Calculate Your MRI (Minimum Required Income) This isn't your dream budget. It's the rock-bottom amount you need to survive. Getting crystal clear on this number is like having GPS coordinates for your destination.

Step 2: Create Your Bucket List
This becomes your reward system and your North Star. It trains your brain to think like an entrepreneur instead of an employee.

Step 3: Retrain Your Brain with a Side Hustle Start earning money outside your day job. This isn't just about extra cash - it's about rewiring how you think about creating income.

Step 4: Kill Your Debt with the Debt Snowball Debt is the anchor keeping you tied to your job. We use the psychological power of small wins to eliminate it fast.

Step 5: Build Your Freedom Engines (Passive Income) This is where the magic happens. Create income streams that pay you whether you work or not.

Step 6: Hit Your Freedom Day (125% of MRI) When your passive income reaches 125% of your minimum required income, you've made it. Work becomes optional.

Step 7: Decide Whether to Quit Your Job Just because you can quit doesn't mean you should. We'll help you make the right choice for your situation.

Step 8: Live the Freedom Day Lifestyle This is about living with intention, using your bucket list as your guide to a purposeful life.

Why the Order Matters

Here's what I learned the hard way: You can't skip steps.

During my pre-pandemic 80-hour weeks, I was trying to do everything at once. Build passive income while carrying massive debt. Create side hustles without knowing my real numbers. Start businesses without a clear destination.

It was chaos.

The Freedom Day Method works because each step builds on the previous one. Your MRI gives you a target. Your bucket list gives you motivation. Your side hustle gives you confidence. Debt elimination gives you freedom to invest. And so on.

Try to skip ahead and you'll end up like I was - working harder but getting nowhere.

The Proof Is in the Results

Since developing this method, I've seen regular people achieve extraordinary results:

- A nurse who built a real estate portfolio that replaced her hospital income
- A software engineer who created an online course business while keeping his day job
- A single mom who turned her baking hobby into a six-figure business

None of them had special advantages. They just followed the steps in order.

Your Blueprint Starts Now

The pandemic taught me that life can change overnight. But instead of waiting for the world to force change on you, why not take control?

The Freedom Day Method isn't just theory. It's the exact system I used to go from working 80-hour weeks to having a work-optional lifestyle.

It's the same system that's helped hundreds of others break free from the retirement trap.

The only question is: Are you ready to start?

Because I can give you the best roadmap in the world, but it only works if you actually follow it.

Your Freedom Day is waiting. Let's go get it.

Freedom Day Story – Alex Edwards

When Life Gives You Lemons...Buy Real Estate

Alex Edwards's story is one of determination and strategic financial growth. Growing up in Dorchester, Boston, he took a first-time homebuyer class in high school, which set the stage for his future in real estate.

After working at Bank of America and learning about mortgages, Edwards bought his first investment property in college at age 20. This ambitious move led him to choose between his education and managing his mortgage, ultimately deciding to focus on his real estate venture.

Despite facing financial challenges and a skyrocketing adjustable-rate mortgage, Edwards creatively navigated his circumstances. He filed for bankruptcy and modified his loan, significantly reducing his mortgage payments and transforming his property into a profitable investment. These decisions allowed him to quit his nine-to-five job, emphasizing his message about the importance of taking calculated risks and believing in oneself.

Alex decided he wanted a career in real estate and went on to delve into different aspects of the industry. He became a real estate agent during the 2008 financial crisis, finding innovative ways to market himself and establish connections. After a successful career as an agent, Alex has become a broker, founding Thumbprint Realty and expanding its reach across multiple states.

His story highlights the significance of resilience, innovative thinking, and the power of real estate investment in achieving financial freedom.

Check out my interview with Alex on our companion site at https://www.FreedomDayMethod.com.

Chapter Homework

As you embark on this journey with the Freedom Day Method, beginning with a clear understanding of your current situation and aspirations is crucial. This chapter's exercises are designed to help you lay the groundwork for achieving your Freedom Day. Please take the time to answer the following questions thoughtfully:

1. Reflect on Your Current Path:

- What aspects of your current lifestyle do you enjoy, and which do you wish to change?
- How does your current job align with your personal values and life goals?

2. Visualize Your Ideal Freedom Day:

- Imagine your perfect day once you've achieved your Freedom Day. What are you doing? Who are you with? Where are you?

3. Commit to the Process:

- Which of the 8 steps feels most challenging to you right now, and why?
- What's one small action you can take this week to begin Step 1 (calculating your MRI)?

Chapter Nine

Freedom Day Method Step 1 - Calculating Your MRI - The Key to Financial Clarity

I'm going to let you in on a secret that changed everything for me.

For years, I thought I was good with money. I made decent income. I paid my bills. I even saved some cash each month.

But I had no clue what my real numbers were.

No idea what I actually *needed* to survive versus what I *wanted* to spend.

That ignorance kept me trapped in jobs I hated and businesses that weren't working. Because I didn't know my real baseline, I couldn't see a path to freedom.

Everything changed when I finally calculated my MRI - my Minimum Required Income.

Why Most People Stay Trapped

Here's the brutal truth: Most people have no idea what it actually costs them to live.

They know what they spend. But they don't know what they *need* to spend.

There's a massive difference.

Your spending includes all the stuff that makes you feel good but doesn't keep you alive. Your MRI is the rock-bottom number that covers your actual survival needs.

Knowing this number is like having GPS coordinates for your Freedom Day destination.

Without it, you're driving blind.

My Credit Card Budgeting Strategy (Yes, Really)

I know what you're thinking. "Jeff, credit cards are evil. Dave Ramsey and Suze Orman would have my head!"

Hear me out.

I use my credit card as a budgeting tool. Every expense goes on the card. Then at the end of the month, I review exactly where every dollar went.

Here's why this works better than cash:

You capture EVERY expense automatically. No guessing. No missing receipts. Everything is tracked digitally.

I pay the card off twice a month to avoid interest. Why twice? Most billing cycles are 30-32 days, not 30. By paying every two weeks, I never get caught by the timing.

Plus, I earn 1-3% cashback on everything. That adds up, especially for business expenses.

The Real Game-Changer

But here's the magic: This system forces you to face reality.

When you see $1,200 at restaurants last month, you can't pretend you "hardly ever eat out."

When you see $400 on random Amazon purchases, you can't claim you "don't buy unnecessary stuff."

The numbers don't lie.

My Debt Wake-Up Call

I learned this lesson the hard way in 2016 when I quit my corporate job to start my businesses.

Crystal and I made a huge mistake. We kept living at the same level as when I had my old job, thinking I'd make the same money as an entrepreneur.

I didn't.

But we kept spending like we had that corporate income. Nice dinners out. Upgrades to the house. All the stuff we were used to.

We went deeper and deeper into debt until we finally ran out of credit. That's when reality smacked us in the face.

We had no choice but to tear our budget down to bare minimum survival level. We sold furniture, tools, books - anything we could find - to create income and pay down debt.

That's when I first calculated what would become my MRI concept. We figured out exactly what we needed to survive versus what we'd been spending.

The result? We paid off over $75,000 in debt in less than 24 months.

But more importantly, I learned the difference between needs and wants. Once we got out of our financial troubles, we kept our spending just slightly above that MRI level.

That discipline allowed us to stay out of debt and build the foundation for everything that followed. That knowledge became the cornerstone of the Freedom Day Method.

What MRI Really Means

Your Minimum Required Income isn't your total earnings. It's the least amount you need to keep the lights on and your family fed.

Think of it as your financial baseline.

This number becomes your target for passive income. When your Freedom Engines generate 125% of your MRI, you've reached Freedom Day.

Why 125%? Because life happens. That extra 25% gives you a buffer for surprises and a little breathing room.

The Power of Knowing Your Number

Once you know your MRI, everything changes.

You stop panicking about losing your job because you know exactly what you need to replace.

You can make calculated decisions about side hustles and passive income because you have a clear target.

You can take risks because you understand the real downside.

Most importantly, you realize that Freedom Day might be closer than you think.

How to Calculate Your MRI

Here's the simple process:

Step 1: Track Everything for One Month Use whatever method works - credit card, debit card, or apps like EveryDollar or Mint. The key is capturing every single expense.

Step 2: Categorize as "Needs" vs "Wants"Be brutally honest here. Netflix might feel like a need, but it's a want. Your mortgage payment? That's a need.

Step 3: Add Up Your Needs This total is your MRI. Everything else is lifestyle enhancement.

Why This Changes Everything

Understanding your MRI is like turning on the lights in a dark room.

Suddenly you can see the path forward clearly.

You know exactly how much passive income you need to build. You understand what you can cut if times get tough. You have a real target instead of a vague dream.

The Tools That Make It Easy

I use EveryDollar (about $99 per year) because it uses zero-based budgeting. Every dollar gets allocated at the beginning of each month.

But you don't need fancy software. A yellow legal pad works fine. So does a simple spreadsheet.

We have a free MRI calculator on our companion website at www.FreedomDayMethod.com/book if you want to try that.

Your Financial Reality Check

Here's what I want you to understand: Your MRI will probably be lower than you think.

When you strip away all the extras and focus on true survival needs, most people discover they can live on 60-70% of what they currently spend.

That's not about living like a monk. It's about understanding the difference between what you need and what you want.

Once you know that difference, you can make conscious choices about both.

The Foundation for Everything Else

Every other step in the Freedom Day Method builds on your MRI.

Your bucket list goals become rewards for hitting income milestones.

Your debt elimination strategy focuses on freeing up cash to invest.

Your passive income targets aim for 125% of this number.

Without a solid MRI, you're building on quicksand.

Time to Face the Music

I get it. Looking at your real numbers can be scary.

But here's the truth: The numbers exist whether you look at them or not.

Ignoring them doesn't make them go away. It just keeps you trapped.

Face the music now, and six months from now you'll be amazed at how much clearer your path to Freedom Day becomes.

Your MRI is your North Star. Everything else navigates around it.

Ready to find out what that number is?

Freedom Day Story – Kim Daly

What you do now may not be what you thought you would do.

Kim Daly's story is an inspiring journey of adjustment and exploration into a different field than originally thought. Initially aspiring to a medical career, Daly's path changed when she discovered the world of franchising. Her early experiences in this field led her to become an entrepreneur, starting her own company at 23. Despite the challenges and loneliness of entrepreneurship, Daly's resilience led her back to franchise consulting, where she found her true passion.

Now, Kim works with FranChoice, helping others become franchisees. Her role involves:

- Guiding candidates through the complexities of franchising.
- Matching them with suitable opportunities.
- Assisting them in making educated decisions.

Kim's approach combines emotional and logical aspects, helping candidates navigate fears and assumptions.

Kim's impact on the franchising world is significant. She has broken industry records, elevating the consultant opportunity. Her story is a testament to the power of adapting to change, leveraging personal experiences, and the importance of mentorship in professional growth.

Check out the full interview with Kim about her story and her secrets behind selecting a franchise at our companion site: https://www.FreedomDayMethod.com/videos

Chapter Homework Assignment: Crafting Your Budget with the MRI Template

Step 1: Visit the Companion Website Go to https://www.FreedomDayMethod.com/book to access the companion resources for "Overcoming The Retirement Trap."

Step 2: Download the MRI Template Locate and download the MRI (Minimum Required Income) template provided on the website. This tool is designed to help you categorize and understand your financial situation better.

Step 3: Gather Your Financial Data Collect all your financial statements, including credit card statements, bank statements, bills, and any other records of your expenses and income.

Step 4: Track Your Expenses Start by listing all your expenses for the past month. If you've been using your credit card, as suggested in the book, you can easily reference your statements to track every expense. Otherwise, manually compile the data from your collected financial documents.

Categorize your expenses into "Needs" and "Wants." Be honest about which expenses are essential (Needs) and which are discretionary (Wants).

Step 5: Calculate Your MRI Sum up all your "Needs" using the template to find your Minimum Required Income. This is the bare minimum you need each month to cover essential expenses.

Optionally, add your "Wants" to understand the full scope of your monthly spending and to identify areas where you might be able to cut back.

Step 6: Review and Adjust Your Spending Analyze your spending categories to identify potential savings. Look for patterns or areas where you might be overspending and consider ways to reduce these costs.

Step 7: Set Financial Goals Set realistic savings, debt reduction, and investing goals based on your MRI and financial analysis. Consider what adjustments you need to make to your spending to meet these goals. These goals may come into play in the next chapter as we set Bucket List Goals.

Step 8: Implement a Strategy for Monitoring and Updating Your Budget Decide on a method for regularly tracking your expenses and income. You can use online tools like Mint.com, EveryDollar, PocketMoney, or simply a spreadsheet.

Schedule a monthly budget review to adjust for any changes in your financial situation or to reflect progress towards your goals.

Step 9: Reflect on Your Financial Reality Take some time to reflect on your current financial situation and how it aligns with your long-term goals. Consider what changes or strategies you need to implement to move closer to financial independence and your Freedom Day.

Chapter Ten

Freedom Day Method Step 2 - Creating Your Bucket List

Sometimes you need to hit rock bottom to find your true direction.

That's exactly what happened to me in 2022 at a conference in Ojai, California.

But this story actually starts a week earlier, back home in Cedar Park, Texas.

The Conversation That Changed Everything

I was having a beer with my business partner at our local brew pub, thinking it was just another casual catch-up meeting.

Then he dropped the bomb: He wanted to buy me out of our firm.

I felt like I'd been punched in the gut. After all we'd built together, he wanted to take the business in a completely different direction than the Freedom Day concepts I'd been developing.

A week later, I found myself on a plane to that conference in Ojai, still reeling from the conversation.

Here I was, thousands of miles from home, in a beautiful resort in one of the most stunning places I'd ever visited. But all I could think about was that my professional world had just exploded.

Four Days to Figure Out My Future

Crystal couldn't come to the conference with me, so I was completely alone with my thoughts.

I had meetings in the mornings, but the rest of each day was my own. No clients to call, no urgent emails to answer. Just me, a beautiful resort, and a whole lot of uncertainty about what came next.

I didn't know a soul at the event. I wasn't in the mood to socialize.

So I did something I rarely do - I stopped. I sat still. I spent those long afternoons thinking about what I actually wanted from life now that my business partnership was ending.

That's when I attended a session by Ben Nemtin, known as the "Bucket List Guy."

The Aha Moment That Completed the Freedom Day Method

Ben talked about how he discovered bucket lists during a difficult time in his own life. How creating a list of dreams and goals became his lifesaver when everything else was falling apart.

Sitting in that conference room, I had my aha moment.

This wasn't just about me figuring out what to do next. This was the missing piece of the Freedom Day Method I'd been developing.

I realized that bucket lists should be part of everyone's Freedom Day Blueprint. They could serve as a reward system along the journey AND become a guiding light after you reach Freedom Day.

I'd been so focused on the financial mechanics of freedom that I'd forgotten about the life you build with that freedom.

That night, I decided to spend the rest of those four days creating my first bucket list and figuring out how to integrate this concept into everything I'd been teaching.

The List That Changed My Life

I spent hours writing down everything I'd ever wanted to do, see, experience, or accomplish.

Some items were small and simple. Others were massive stretch goals that seemed impossible.

But something magical happened as I wrote. For the first time in months, I started feeling excited about the future instead of anxious about it.

That bucket list became my roadmap for the next phase of my life. It helped me realize what I truly valued and what direction I wanted to go.

More importantly, it gave me a framework for the months that followed as I navigated selling my business and transitioning to my Freedom Day.

Why Bucket Lists Are Essential for Freedom Day

Here's what most people don't understand about bucket lists: They're not just dream boards or feel-good exercises.

They're strategic tools for financial independence.

Your bucket list serves three critical purposes in the Freedom Day Method:

Purpose 1: Retraining Your BrainA bucket list forces you to shift from employee thinking ("I can't afford that") to entrepreneur thinking ("How can I afford that?").

That mental shift is the difference between staying trapped and breaking free.

Purpose 2: Reward System Your bucket list becomes your motivation system. Instead of depriving yourself for 30 years to retire, you reward yourself for hitting milestones along the way.

Purpose 3: Life After Freedom Day Once you reach Freedom Day, your bucket list becomes your guide for living intentionally. It prevents you from falling into the "now what?" trap that hits many people after they achieve financial independence.

The System That Works

Ben Nemtin taught me to organize bucket list goals into ten categories:

1. **Travel and Adventure Goals** - Places to go, experiences to have
2. **Giving Goals** - Ways to help others and give back
3. **Intellectual Goals** - Things to learn and study
4. **Material Goals** - Things you want to own (be honest here)
5. **Financial Goals** - Money milestones to hit
6. **Creative Goals** - Art, music, writing, building
7. **Professional Goals** - Career achievements and business goals
8. **Relationship Goals** - Connections to build and deepen
9. **Health Goals** - Physical challenges and wellness targets
10. **Mental Health Goals** - Emotional and spiritual growth

The goal is ten items in each category. That gives you 100 dreams to chase.

My First Bucket List Win

The first thing I checked off my list happened that very week in Ojai.

I'd written: "Have a private concert with the Eagles, my favorite band."

I thought this was completely impossible. Just a crazy dream I threw on the list, never thinking it would actually happen.

On the final night of the conference, they surprised us with a special event that included a private concert featuring Don Felder - one of the original Eagles and the writer of my favorite song of all time, "Hotel California."

I couldn't believe it. Thanks for that one, universe!

Not the whole band, but close enough. I immediately checked that one off my bucket list and took it as proof that putting dreams out into the universe actually works.

The Magic of Writing It Down

Something powerful happens when you write down your dreams.

They stop being fantasies and start becoming possibilities.

Since creating my first bucket list in 2022, I've checked off over 30 goals and replaced them with new ones.

I've driven an Aston Martin at Silverstone F1 track, flown in a B-25 Mitchell bomber, ridden the largest steam locomotive still functioning, and dozens of other adventures.

Each one cost around $500. But instead of putting them on a credit card, I created income streams to fund them.

Your Freedom Day Fuel

Your bucket list isn't just about fun and games. It's fuel for your Freedom Day journey.

When you're grinding through debt elimination or building passive income streams, your bucket list reminds you why you're doing all this work.

It keeps you focused on living life, not just surviving it.

Getting Started Right Now

Here's what I want you to do:

Download the free bucket list worksheet from our companion website at https://www.FreedomDayMethod.com/book.

Start with just one category that excites you most. Don't worry about filling all ten categories perfectly.

Then pick three goals you can achieve in the next six months for under $500 each.

These become your first rewards as you work through the Freedom Day Method.

The Life You're Really Building

Your bucket list isn't separate from your financial plan. It IS your financial plan.

Every goal teaches you something about creating income, managing money, or investing in experiences.

More importantly, it ensures that your journey to Freedom Day is about building a life worth living, not just accumulating money.

Remember: You're not just planning for financial independence. You're planning for a life of intention, adventure, and purpose.

That life starts with a list.

Freedom Day Story – Roger Williams, "Chief Crosser Over"

Living La Vida Bucket List

Roger Williams' inspiring journey began during the pandemic. As a guidance counselor working with high school students, he missed the personal interaction with his students that was lost during the pandemic.

Being trapped in a small apartment in Seattle during the pandemic led Roger to plan a Bucket List of things he wanted to do after the pandemic. Having a life-altering heart attack in 2020 made him rethink his life. This event catalyzed change, leading him to take an "Adult Gap Year" and actively pursue his bucket list dreams.

Among his Bucket List Goals, the most challenging and rewarding was the Camino de Santiago, a historic 790-kilometer pilgrimage across Northern Spain. Roger completed this trek despite facing initial obstacles, like having a heart attack six months before he was supposed to leave, symbolizing his new approach to life.

His story is more than just about accomplishing goals; it's a testament to the power of resilience and the importance of seizing the moment and living life to the fullest. More than anything, however, Roger realized that his bucket list journey was more than just checking things off of a list. It had meaning (for him, it was community).

Roger's experience encourages others not to wait for the right moment but to create it, embracing life's adventures with enthusiasm and determination.

One of Roger's bucket list items was to write a book about his journey. His book "Live Out Your List: Finding Joy Through A Bucket List Lifestyle" and his podcast, "The Crossing it Off Podcast," are two things I recommend most for people starting their Freedom Day Journey.

> Check out the Full Interview with Roger on our companion site: https://www.FreedomDayMethod.com/videos.

Chapter Homework

Now is the time to get to work and create a personalized bucket list, a powerful way to visualize and plan for a life filled with rich experiences, achievements, and personal growth. Utilizing the Bucket List worksheet available on our companion website, https://www.FreedomDayMethod.com/book.

I encourage you to dream big and set intentions across ten distinct categories. Each category should contain ten goals, culminating in a comprehensive list of 100 goals.

Below is a brief explanation of each category and suggestions for the goals you might consider.

1. Travel and Adventure Goals Explanation: This category is for exploring new places, cultures, and experiences that invigorate your sense of adventure.

Goal Suggestions: Visit the Great Wall of China, skydive in Dubai, backpack through Europe, see the Northern Lights, or take a safari in Africa.

2. Giving Goals Explanation: Focus on philanthropy, volunteering, and making a difference in the lives of others or the environment.

Goal Suggestions: Volunteer in a foreign country, start a scholarship fund, plant a thousand trees, or contribute to a cause you're passionate about.

3. Intellectual Goals Explanation: Learning, education, and mental expansion goals.

Goal Suggestions: Learn a new language, earn a degree or certification, read 100 classic novels, or attend a prestigious workshop or seminar.

4. Material Goals Explanation: Aspirations for acquiring specific material possessions that bring you joy or fulfill a personal desire.

Goal Suggestions: Own your dream home, purchase a vintage car, acquire an original piece of art, or own a luxury watch.

5. Financial Goals Explanation: Objectives that focus on financial security, independence, and wealth-building.

Goal Suggestions: Achieve a net worth of X amount, retire by 50, create a successful investment portfolio, or become debt-free.

6. Creative Goals Explanation: Goals that nurture your creativity and artistic expression.

Goal Suggestions: Write a novel, record a song, have an art exhibit, or design a piece of furniture.

7. Professional Goals Explanation: Aspirations related to your career, business, or professional development.

Goal Suggestions: Start your own business, become a CEO, earn a prestigious award in your field, or mentor young professionals.

8. Relationship Goals Explanation: Objectives focused on building, nurturing, or restoring relationships.

Goal Suggestions: Renew wedding vows in a romantic location, have family reunions, make a new friend every year, or resolve a longstanding conflict.

9. Health Goals Explanation: Goals dedicated to improving physical health, fitness, and well-being.

Goal Suggestions: Run a marathon, achieve your ideal weight, complete a triathlon, or climb a significant mountain.

10. Mental Health Goals Explanation: Aim to enhance your emotional well-being, resilience, and mental health.

Goal Suggestions: Practice daily meditation for a year, attend a silent retreat, master stress management techniques, or complete a mindfulness course.

Setting goals across these ten categories ensures a balanced approach to personal fulfillment and growth. The idea is not just to dream but to create a diversified plan that touches all aspects of life, encouraging you to live fully and intentionally. Use the Bucket List worksheet as a dynamic tool to revisit and update your goals as you grow and evolve to overcome the retirement trap.

Chapter Eleven

Freedom Day Method Step 3 - Retraining Your Brain for Financial Success

Sometimes the most important lessons come from the moments when you have absolutely no choice but to figure it out.

Let me take you back to month 17 of my entrepreneurial journey. The month when everything almost fell apart.

When Reality Hits Hard

Remember, I quit my job in 2016 with grand plans of building successful businesses. I thought I'd make the same money as an entrepreneur that I'd made as an employee.

I was spectacularly wrong.

Seventeen months in, Crystal and I were broke. Not "a little tight on cash" broke. Actually broke.

The coworking space was hemorrhaging money. The wealth management practice was just beginning to grow but wasn't making enough to pay our bills.

We'd burned through our savings. We'd maxed out credit cards. We were digging up change around the house to buy groceries.

I had two choices: Give up on my businesses and go back to corporate life, or find a way to generate immediate cash while keeping the businesses alive.

I chose to fight.

That meant doing whatever it took to bring in money. So I downloaded the Uber and food delivery apps and started driving.

The Appeal of the Gig Economy

At first, driving for Uber and doing food delivery felt like a lifeline. I could set my own schedule and work around my business commitments. Need $50 today? Drive for a few hours. Have a big client meeting? No problem, just don't log into the app.

The flexibility was exactly what I needed during those chaotic early business days.

But there was a massive problem I didn't see coming: I was trading time for money, and not very much money at that.

After gas, wear and tear on my car, and taxes, I was making about $8 an hour. Maybe $10 on a really good day.

The Time Trap

As my businesses slowly started to take off, I found myself in an impossible situation. The more successful my real businesses became, the less time I had for driving.

But I still needed the delivery income to keep us afloat.

I was trapped between two competing demands: My businesses needed more of my time to grow, but I needed the driving income to survive.

There literally weren't enough hours in the day.

The Groundhog Day from Hell

That's when my schedule became a nightmare loop:

4:00 AM - Drive people to the airport through Uber8:00 AM - Work on my businesses all day6:00 PM - Food delivery and rideshare until I hit my daily goal

I set a goal of making $200 a day through driving. Some days I'd make more, but hitting that number often meant working 7 days a week.

Sometimes I didn't get home until midnight or later. No breaks. No vacations.

After gas, wear and tear, and taxes, I was making about $8 an hour. It was soul-crushing work, but it kept us alive.

Selling Everything That Wasn't Nailed Down

The Uber money wasn't enough. So we started selling everything we could.

Woodworking tools. Video games. Furniture. Electronics.

The most painful was selling my books. I'm a reader, and my personal library was one of my most treasured possessions. Watching those boxes of books disappear felt like selling pieces of my soul.

But we needed cash more than we needed stuff.

The Moment Everything Shifted

After 14 months of this insane schedule, I hit a wall. My businesses were finally starting to make money, but they were taking more of my time. That left less time for Uber and food delivery.

I was trapped. I couldn't squeeze more hours out of the day, but I needed more money.

That's when I had the realization that changed everything:

Selling time for money doesn't scale. There will never be enough hours in the day.

I had to find a way to make more money per hour. I had to work smarter, not just harder.

The Skill That Saved Me

I took inventory of what I was actually good at. One skill stood out: writing business plans.

During my corporate days, I'd become an expert at creating business plans that helped clients get bank financing. It was a valuable skill that most people didn't have.

So I created a profile on Upwork and started offering business plan services.

At first, I charged dirt cheap - about $100 per plan. Each plan took me about 10 hours, so I was making $10 an hour. Still better than Uber.

But here's where it gets interesting.

The Breakthrough That Changed Everything

As I got better reviews and more experience, I could charge more. I also started systematizing the process.

I created templates. I developed procedures. I figured out how to do research faster.

Then I hired Raj, a brilliant MBA graduate in India with perfect English skills.

Here's what we figured out together:

- Total time per business plan: 6 hours
- My time: 2 hours (initial consultation and final presentation)
- Raj's time: 4 hours (research and assembly)

- Our fee: $2,000 per plan
- Split evenly: $1,000 each
- My rate: $1,000 for 2 hours of work = $500 per hour

This wasn't just a side hustle anymore. This was passive income.

The Real Brain Training

But here's what I really learned during those dark months:

The shift from employee thinking to entrepreneur thinking isn't just about starting a business. It's about completely rewiring how you approach problems.

Employee Brain says:

- "I can't afford that"
- "I don't have time"
- "I need to ask permission"
- "Someone should pay me more"

Entrepreneur Brain says:

- "How can I afford that?"
- "How can I create time?"
- "How can I make this happen?"
- "How can I create more value?"

That shift in questions changes everything.

Your Side Hustle Is Brain Training

When I tell people to start a side hustle, I'm not just talking about making extra money.

I'm talking about retraining your brain to think like an entrepreneur instead of an employee.

Every time you figure out how to solve a client's problem, you're training your brain to create value instead of just trading time.

Every time you set your own prices, you're training your brain to think about worth instead of wages.

Every time you find a customer, you're training your brain to create opportunities instead of waiting for them.

The Mindset That Changes Everything

Here's the difference that matters:

When your car breaks down and needs $1,200 in repairs, what's your first thought?

Employee brain: "I can't afford this. I guess I'll put it on a credit card."

Entrepreneur brain: "How can I make $1,200 this month to pay for this?"

That shift in thinking is what separates people who stay trapped from people who break free.

Finding Your Skill

You don't need to be an expert to start. You just need to know something that other people don't know.

Can you edit videos? There are businesses that need that.Are you good at organizing? Busy executives will pay for that.Do you understand social media? Local businesses are desperate for help.Can you write clearly? Everyone needs content.

The easiest way to get started is through platforms like Upwork.com or Fiverr.com. These sites connect freelancers with clients who need specific services. You can create a profile, showcase your skills, and start bidding on projects immediately.

The goal isn't to find the perfect side hustle. The goal is to start thinking like someone who creates income instead of someone who waits to receive it.

Your Three Bucket List Goals

Remember those three goals from your bucket list that cost under $500 each?

Use your side hustle income to fund them. Not your day job income. Not your savings. Not a credit card.

Earn that money through your own effort, then reward yourself.

This creates a powerful psychological connection between entrepreneurial thinking and the life you want to live.

The Path Forward

Your side hustle isn't just about extra money. It's about proving to yourself that you can create income when you need it.

That confidence changes everything.

When you know you can make money, you stop being afraid of losing money. When you stop being afraid, you start taking the calculated risks that lead to real wealth.

The brain retraining starts now. Not when you're ready. Not when you have time. Not when conditions are perfect.

Now.

Because the only difference between where you are and where you want to be is the story you tell yourself about what's possible.

Time to change that story.

Freedom Day Story – Elizabeth Eisse

What it takes to be a successful Freelancer

Elizabeth Eisse's story is an inspiring narrative of her transition from the corporate world to entrepreneurship. Starting in the insurance industry, Elizabeth developed a diverse skill set in commercial risk underwriting and technology. Her career trajectory took a significant turn when she joined a startup focusing on expertise location using technology. Despite the startup's failure, Elizabeth's entrepreneurial spirit flourished, leading her to consult for other early-stage companies.

The pivotal moment in Elizabeth's journey was her experience hiring freelancers to supplement her expertise. This experience sparked the idea for her current venture, a matchmaking platform for freelance talent focusing on solopreneurs and small to mid-sized businesses. Her platform, designed to include human interaction in the freelancer hiring process, showcases her commitment to helping companies thrive by finding the right talent. Elizabeth's story exemplifies the potential for growth and innovation when one embraces change and leverages one's experiences to create new opportunities.

You can watch my full interview with Elizabeth, where she also shares what it takes to become a successful freelancer, on our companion site at https://www.FreedomDayMethod.com/videos.

Chapter Homework

Alright, now is the time for some fun. It is time to start looking for your side hustle. Will it be Uber (I hope not!)? Or will you use some of the skills that you have from work? Maybe it is a hobby that you can convert into income. That is for you to decide. Go to our companion website, https://www.FreedomDayMethod.com, to download our "Side Hustle Brainstorming" sheet, which will help you do some brainstorming. The steps below will also help you get started.

1. Reflect on Your Skills and Interests: Review your bucket list and personal experiences to identify skills or hobbies you enjoy and could potentially monetize.

2. Research and Inspiration: Visit websites like Fiverr (https://www.Fiverr.com) or Upwork (https://www.upwork.com) to explore various services. Look for areas that align with your skills or where you see a demand you can meet. This will give you an idea of the services people are providing and what they are getting paid to do them.

3. Brainstorming Side Hustle Ideas: Using the worksheet, list potential side hustle ideas based on your skills, hobbies, and market research. Aim for a diverse range of options that interest you.

4. Evaluate Feasibility and Impact: For each idea, consider the potential income, the time investment required, and how it aligns with achieving your bucket list goals. Prioritize ideas that seem most viable and enjoyable.

5. Set a Financial Goal: Choose a financial target for your side hustle, such as making your first $500, and decide which bucket list goal this income will help you achieve.

6. Action Plan: For your top side hustle ideas, outline the first few steps needed to start. This might include creating a profile on a freelance platform, setting up a small business website (use sites like Weebly or Wix), or advertising your services locally by setting up a Google My Business Profile.

7. Commit to Starting: Initially, select one side hustle idea to focus on. Commit to taking the first step within the next week to begin your journey towards retraining your brain for financial freedom.

This exercise encourages practical steps towards generating additional income through side hustles, aligning with the overarching goal of financial independence, and achieving some of your Bucket List dreams.

Make a Difference with Your Review

Unlock the Power of Generosity

"Success isn't just about what you accomplish in your life—it's about what you inspire others to do." – Unknown

Helping someone else find their Freedom Day might just be the most rewarding thing you do today.

There are folks out there—just like you—wondering if they'll ever feel ready to retire. Some are burned out. Some are scared to sell their business. Others are just looking for a way to stop working *because they want to,* not because they have to.

That's why I wrote *Overcoming the Retirement Trap*—to make retirement feel possible, simple, and even exciting again. But to reach more people, I need your help.

Most people find books through reviews. If this book helped you at all, even a little, would you take one minute to leave a review?

Your review could help...

...one more family create a real plan.
...one more business owner sell on their terms.

...one more person believe that retirement *can* work.
...one more dream turn into a Freedom Day.

To make a difference, just scan the QR code or visit:
https://www.amazon.com/review/review-your-purchases/?asin=B0FD5DMQ54

If you care about helping others—you're my kind of person.

Thank you from the bottom of my heart,
Jeff Kikel

Chapter Twelve

Freedom Day Method Step 4 - Kill Your Debt with The Debt Snowball Method

The credit card statement felt like a death sentence in my hands.

I remember sitting at our kitchen table one evening in 2008, surrounded by a mountain of bills, staring at numbers that seemed impossible. Crystal and I had somehow accumulated over $30,000 in credit card debt, and for the first time in our lives, we were drowning.

When Credit Cards Became Our Drug Dealer

Let me take you back to how we got here, because our story might sound familiar.

I grew up in a family that never talked about money. We had enough to get by, but personal finances, budgeting, and debt management were never dinner table conversations. School didn't teach me much about real-world finances either.

So when Crystal and I started our adult lives together, credit cards felt like magic. Need furniture for our new apartment? Put it on the card. Want to take a vacation? Card. Car repairs? Card.

Credit became like having a rich uncle who kept giving us money. The minimum payments seemed manageable, and we told ourselves we'd pay them off "someday when we made more money."

The harder we worked, the more we earned, the more we spent. It was an endless cycle that we couldn't see was slowly strangling our financial future.

The Day the Music Stopped

Then 2008 happened.

The financial crisis hit, and suddenly our "rich uncle" credit card companies stopped being so generous. Credit limits were slashed. Interest rates skyrocketed. New credit became impossible to get.

For the first time, we were forced to face the monster we'd created.

I'll never forget the night I finally calculated our total debt. Over $30,000 spread across multiple cards, with minimum payments that were bleeding us dry every month.

Crystal looked at me with tears in her eyes and said, "How did we let this happen?"

I didn't have an answer. All I knew was that we were trapped, and I had no idea how to get out.

The Discovery That Changed Everything

That's when a friend recommended Dave Ramsey's book "The Total Money Makeover."

I was skeptical. Another financial guru promising easy solutions? But we were desperate enough to try anything.

What I discovered in that book wasn't just a strategy – it was a lifeline.

Dave's approach was different. He understood the psychology of debt, the shame, the feeling of being trapped. But more importantly, he had a clear, step-by-step plan that felt achievable.

The Debt Snowball Method became our battle plan.

Our Debt Snowball Victory

The concept was brilliantly simple: List all your debts from smallest to largest, regardless of interest rates. Pay minimum payments on everything, but attack the smallest debt with every extra dollar you can find.

When that smallest debt is gone, take the money you were paying on it and add it to the payment for the next smallest debt. Like a snowball rolling downhill, your payments get bigger and more powerful with each debt you eliminate.

Here's what our journey looked like:

Month 1-3: We cut our expenses significantly and lived like we were broke (because we were). Every extra dollar went to the smallest debt.

Month 4: First victory! We paid off our smallest credit card. The psychological boost was incredible. For the first time in years, we felt hope.

Month 6: Second card gone. The snowball was rolling.

Month 12: Three more cards eliminated. We could see the light at the end of the tunnel.

Month 18: The final payment. We were debt-free.

The results were life-changing. Our cash flow improved by almost $2,000 per month. But more than the money, we felt free. The weight of debt that had been crushing us for years was finally gone.

Why the Debt Snowball Works

Critics of the Debt Snowball argue that you should pay off high-interest debt first to save money mathematically. They're not wrong about the math.

But debt elimination isn't just about math – it's about psychology.

The Debt Snowball Method works because:

Quick Wins Build Momentum: Paying off that first small debt gives you an immediate victory. You see progress quickly, which motivates you to keep going.

Simplified Focus: Instead of juggling complex calculations about interest rates, you have a clear, simple plan to follow.

Behavioral Change: The method retrains your brain to see debt elimination as achievable rather than overwhelming.

Sustainable Motivation: Each paid-off debt provides positive reinforcement, making it easier to stick with the plan.

The difference between the lowest-cost mathematical approach and the Debt Snowball is usually minimal, but the difference in completion rates is massive. The best debt elimination plan is the one you'll actually finish.

Understanding Good Debt vs. Bad Debt

Not all debt is created equal. Understanding the difference between "good debt" and "bad debt" is crucial for your financial journey.

Good Debt: Investments in Your Future

Good debt typically appreciates in value or helps you build wealth over time:

- **Mortgages:** Real estate generally appreciates, and homeownership builds equity
- **Student Loans:** Education increases your earning potential (though this is debatable in today's economy)
- **Business Loans:** Can generate income and build assets

Bad Debt: The Wealth Killers

Bad debt drains your wealth and doesn't improve your financial position:

- **Credit Card Debt:** High interest rates on depreciating purchases
- **Car Loans:** Vehicles lose value the moment you drive them off the lot
- **Personal Loans for Consumption:** Borrowing for vacations, clothes, or gadgets

Our Strategy: Focus on eliminating all bad debt first using the Debt Snowball. Hold off on paying extra toward good debt (like your mortgage) until your cash flow is freed up from bad debt payments.

The Debt Snowball in Action

Ready to start your own debt elimination journey? Here's how to implement the Debt Snowball Method:

Step 1: List All Your Debts Write down every debt you owe (except your mortgage):

- Creditor name
- Total balance owed
- Minimum monthly payment
- Interest rate

Step 2: Order by Balance Arrange your debts from smallest balance to largest, regardless of interest rate.

Step 3: Find Extra Money Look for additional money to throw at debt:

- Cut unnecessary expenses
- Use your side hustle income

- Sell stuff you don't need
- Use tax refunds or bonuses

Step 4: Attack the Smallest Debt Pay minimum payments on all debts, but put every extra dollar toward the smallest debt.

Step 5: Roll Over Payments When the smallest debt is paid off, take the total amount you were paying on it (minimum plus extra) and add it to the minimum payment of the next smallest debt.

Step 6: Repeat Until Free Continue this process until all debts are eliminated.

Your Side Hustle Connection

Remember that side hustle from Step 3? This is where it becomes your secret weapon.

Instead of using side hustle income for bucket list goals while you have debt, temporarily redirect that income toward debt elimination. This accelerates your timeline dramatically.

Once you're debt-free, you can redirect that side hustle income toward your bucket list and passive income goals.

The Psychological Transformation

What we discovered through the Debt Snowball wasn't just financial – it was psychological.

For years, we'd been passengers in our financial lives, letting credit card companies and debt dictate our choices. The Debt Snowball put us back in the driver's seat.

Each paid-off debt was proof that we could take control. We weren't victims of our circumstances – we were agents of change.

That mindset shift was invaluable preparation for building wealth. Once you prove to yourself that you can eliminate debt, building passive income feels achievable rather than impossible.

The Freedom on the Other Side

I can't overstate how different life feels without debt payments.

That $2,000 per month we freed up became our wealth-building engine. Instead of making credit card companies rich, we were making ourselves rich.

But the real freedom was psychological. No more anxiety about minimum payments. No more shame about our financial situation. No more feeling trapped by our past decisions.

We were finally free to build the life we wanted instead of paying for the life we used to live.

Your Debt-Free Future

As we wrap up this chapter, I want you to imagine your life without debt payments.

What would you do with that extra money each month? How would it feel to know that every dollar you earn belongs to you, not to credit card companies?

The Debt Snowball Method isn't just about paying off debt – it's about reclaiming your financial freedom and taking control of your destiny.

Your Freedom Day journey requires this foundation. You can't build lasting wealth while debt is draining your resources.

But here's the good news: if Crystal and I could climb out of a $30,000 debt hole, you can eliminate whatever debt is holding you back.

The snowball starts rolling with your first payment. Are you ready to give it a push?

Freedom Day Story – Reena Friedman Watts

From The Jerry Springer Show to Podcast Success

Reena Friedman Watts's story is an inspiring journey of adaptability, creativity, and success. Starting her career in the dynamic environment of the Jerry Springer show, Reena honed her skills in storytelling and production.

This experience laid the foundation for her diverse career path, including radio and event coordination roles. Reena was looking for a new career after becoming a mom and moving back to Chicago from the West Coast. Going back to her days of booking people on the Springer show, she created a business that helped others get booked on podcasts.

Her business led her to transition into podcasting, leveraging her extensive experience in media and natural networking abilities.

Reena's Better Call Daddy podcast showcases her talent for connecting with people and sharing insightful stories. Her ability to interview and extract unique perspectives from her guests has led to her remarkable success, not to mention the comic relief of bringing her dad on at the end of the show to comment about the episodes (he is hilarious!).

Her story is a testament to the power of embracing change and the importance of nurturing relationships in professional development.

Check out the full interview with Reena on our companion site: https://www.FreedomDayMethod.com/videos.

Chapter Homework: Mastering the Debt Snowball Method

Welcome to a pivotal step in transforming your financial landscape—conquering debt with the Debt Snowball Method. This exercise is designed to move you from understanding to action. By applying what you've learned, you'll see tangible progress in your journey toward financial freedom. This homework will guide you through using the Debt Snowball Spreadsheet, a powerful tool to strategize your debt repayment in a manageable, motivating way.

Instructions:

1. Download the Spreadsheet: Download the Debt Snowball Spreadsheet from our companion website (https://www.FreedomDayMethod.com/book). This tool is your roadmap for debt eradication.

2. List Your Debts: Enter all your debts into the spreadsheet. Start with the creditor's name, balance owed, minimum monthly payment, and interest rate for each debt.

3. Order Your Debts: Organize your debts in ascending order based on the balance owed, from smallest to largest. This sequence is the essence of the Debt Snowball Method.

4. Determine Your Extra Payment: Decide how much extra you can pay toward your smallest monthly debt and the minimum payments on all your debts. Consider incorporating any additional income from side hustles.

5. Apply Your Payments: Using the spreadsheet, allocate your extra payment to the smallest debt while continuing minimum payments on others. Update the spreadsheet as you make payments.

6. Roll Over Payments: Once the smallest debt is paid off, redirect the amount you paid (minimum plus extra) to the next smallest debt. Update the spreadsheet to reflect this new payment strategy.

7. Celebrate Wins: Mark each debt as paid in the spreadsheet once cleared. Celebrate these milestones to maintain motivation.

8. Repeat Until Debt-Free: Continue this process, moving from one debt to the next, until all your debts are paid off. The spreadsheet will visually track your progress and encourage you as you reach your goal.

Conclusion:

This homework is more than just a task; it's a step toward reclaiming your financial independence and making your Freedom Day a reality. By actively applying the Debt Snowball Method, you're not just paying off debt but building a foundation for a future where financial stress is a thing of the past. Let's roll up our sleeves and start making your debts melt away with each snowball you throw.

Chapter Thirteen

Freedom Day Method Step 5 - Transitioning to Passive Income – The Game Changer

There I was at 10 PM, sitting in my car outside a McDonald's, waiting for someone to pick up their DoorDash order. I was exhausted, running on fumes, and staring at my phone calculating whether this $6 delivery would get me closer to my daily goal of making $200.

That's when it hit me like a freight train.

I was trapped. I had gone from a highly paid executive in the Financial Services to this. Completely and utterly trapped in what I now call the "Time Prison."

The Mathematical Prison

Let me show you the horrifying schedule that was killing me. I'd wake up at 4 AM and drive for Uber until 8 AM - that was usually good for about $80. Then I'd rush home, grab coffee, and work on my actual businesses from 8 AM until 5 PM. After a quick dinner, I'd head back out for food delivery and more Uber driving until I hit my $200 daily goal - usually around 10 or 11 PM.

Seven days a week.

That's 19 hours a day with barely any time to breathe, let alone spend with Crystal or take care of myself. I was essentially working two full-time jobs simultaneously - trying to keep my businesses alive while doing whatever it took to pay the bills.

But here's where it gets really scary. Working two full-time jobs at once makes the need for passive income breakthrough even more dramatic.

The story now shows the impossible juggling act that forced me to find a better way.

The Phone Call That Changed Everything

Three weeks into this nightmare schedule, Crystal called me while I was sitting in another parking lot, waiting for another delivery.

"Jeff, this isn't working," she said quietly. "You're killing yourself for $200 a day, and I never see you anymore. There has to be a better way."

She was right. I was trading my life for dollars, and the exchange rate was terrible.

But what was the alternative? I'd already tried seven different businesses. I'd already failed more times than I cared to count. The only thing I knew how to do was work harder, longer, faster.

That's when everything changed.

The Business Plan Breakthrough

Remember Raj from Chapter 11? The business plan partnership that took me from $20 per hour driving to $500 per hour for just 10 hours of work per month?

That night, sitting in my car after Crystal's call, I finally understood what had happened. For the first time in my entrepreneurial journey, I had stopped trading time for money.

When I wrote those business plans, I wasn't getting paid for my time. I was getting paid for my knowledge, my experience, and my ability to create something valuable. Raj handled the client interaction, the revisions, the hand-holding. I just created the blueprint.

Ten hours per month. $5,000 in my pocket. $500 per hour.

That was almost double what I was making driving Uber and delivering food - and I only had to work 10 hours per month instead of 280 hours per month.

That's when I realized I wasn't in the time business anymore. I was in the value business.

From Time Seller to Treasure Hunter

That revelation transformed me from what I call a "time seller" into a "treasure hunter."

Time sellers trade hours for dollars. They're limited by the number of hours they can work, and their income has a ceiling determined by how much someone will pay per hour.

Treasure hunters, on the other hand, seek out opportunities to create value that generates income without requiring their constant presence. They look for ways to make money while they sleep, while they're on vacation, while they're spending time with their families.

I became obsessed with finding these treasures.

The Five Types of Treasure

Over the next few months, I discovered there are essentially five types of passive income "treasures" you can hunt for:

Digital Products - Create once, sell forever. Think online courses, ebooks, software, apps. I started creating business plan templates and selling them online.

Rental Income - Real estate that pays you monthly. We eventually bought rental properties that generated consistent cash flow.

Investment Income - Stocks, bonds, and index funds that pay dividends or appreciate over time. This became our long-term wealth building strategy.

Business Systems - Companies that run without your daily involvement. I systematized my business consulting so it could generate revenue even when I wasn't actively working.

Royalties and Licensing - Getting paid for intellectual property. I started licensing my business frameworks to other consultants.

The beauty of passive income isn't that you never work. It's that you work once and get paid many times.

The Progression Path

Here's what I learned about the journey from active to passive income:

Stage 1: Active Income - You trade time for money. This is where most people stay forever.

Stage 2: Leveraged Income - You get paid more for your time by increasing your value. My Raj partnership was leveraged income.

Stage 3: Semi-Passive Income - You create systems that generate income with minimal ongoing effort. My consulting business became semi-passive.

Stage 4: True Passive Income - Money that comes in whether you work or not. Our rental properties and investment portfolio represent true passive income.

Most people try to jump straight from Stage 1 to Stage 4. That's like trying to bench press 300 pounds on your first day at the gym. You'll get crushed.

The secret is progressing through each stage systematically.

My Current Treasure Map

Today, our household income comes from multiple different sources:

1. Consulting fees (leveraged income)
2. Online course sales (digital products)
3. Rental property income (real estate)
4. Stock dividends and Option Income Strategies (investment income)
5. Business profits many of these with multiple sources of income (business systems)
6. Licensing fees (royalties)
7. Ecommerce Sales (Business Income)
8. Book publishing, Podcasts, Online Media (Business and Royalty Income)

If any one source disappears tomorrow, we'll still be fine. That's the power of diversification. My goal now is to continue to develop out my existing revenue and search out and develop more.

But here's the most important part: none of this would have been possible if I hadn't first escaped the Time Prison.

Freedom Day Story: Scott Jelinek

A Different Approach To The Real Estate Market

Scott Jelinek's story is a testament to resilience and innovation in real estate. After High School, he became a full-time landscaper, which led him to buy his first home. Beginning in 1994 with a traditional property investing approach, Scott accumulated a substantial portfolio of 94 houses.

The 2008 financial crisis, however, was a turning point. After losing 55 properties to foreclosure and having no money or credit, Scott reevaluated his strategy and switched to "slow flips." This approach involved buying properties on short-term, five-year private notes and selling them on longer, 30-year term agreements. The goal was clear: acquire properties with short-term financing, sell them immediately as is with no renovations to someone willing to do the renovations. Then Scott finances the sale with a long term "mortgage" on properties that would usually not qualify for traditional financing. Within 5 years he has an asset paying him monthly payments with no cost to him, just pure profit. Absolute genius.

This strategic shift wasn't just about recovery but a complete reinvention of Scott's business model. He mitigated the risks associated with market volatility by focusing on long-term gains rather than short-term cash flow. By 2022, this new strategy had not only helped him recover from the 2008 crash but had also put him on the path to a sustainable real estate income, with no property management hassles and no need to worry about the economy.

Scott's journey in real estate powerfully illustrates how adaptability and strategic thinking can lead to success, even during economic downturns. His experience provides valuable insights for investors on the importance of flexibility and the need to constantly reassess and refine investment strategies in response to changing market conditions. Today Scott not only continues to invest in "Short Flips", he also teaches others to do the same.

You can watch the full interview with Scott on our companion site, www.FreedomDayMethod.com/videos

Your Treasure Hunt Begins Now

The transition to passive income doesn't happen overnight. It starts with a simple question: "How can I get paid for this more than once?"

Maybe you're a teacher who could create an online course. Maybe you're a craftsperson who could sell digital patterns. Maybe you're a consultant who could license your methodology. Maybe you have savings that could become a down payment on rental property.

The opportunities are everywhere once you start looking with treasure hunter eyes.

Remember, every successful treasure hunter started the same way: broke, tired, and trading time for money. The difference between those who escape the Time Prison and those who don't isn't talent or luck.

It's the decision to stop being a time seller and start being a treasure hunter.

Your Freedom Day depends on it.

Chapter Homework: Designing Your Passive Income Strategy

Objective: To identify your current income situation, explore passive income opportunities, and create a plan to transition from active to passive income streams.

Instructions:

Step 1: Assess Your Current Income Stage Using the four-stage progression from the chapter, identify where you currently stand:

- Stage 1: Active Income (trading time for money)

- Stage 2: Leveraged Income (getting paid more for your time)
- Stage 3: Semi-Passive Income (systems with minimal ongoing effort)
- Stage 4: True Passive Income (money that comes in whether you work or not)

Write down your current stage and what percentage of your income comes from each stage.

Step 2: Calculate Your "Time Prison" Score Document your current time-for-money situation:

- How many hours per week do you work for your primary income?
- What's your effective hourly rate after expenses?
- How many hours could you realistically work per week maximum?
- What's your income ceiling if you maxed out your hours?

Step 3: Identify Your Treasure Type Review the five types of passive income "treasures" and rank them 1-5 based on your interest and current skills:

- Digital Products (courses, ebooks, software, apps)
- Rental Income (real estate investments)
- Investment Income (stocks, bonds, dividends)
- Business Systems (companies that run without you)
- Royalties and Licensing (intellectual property)

Step 4: Brainstorm Your Passive Income Ideas For your top-ranked treasure type, brainstorm 3-5 specific ideas:

- What knowledge, skills, or assets do you have that others would pay for repeatedly?
- What problems do you solve that you could systematize?
- What do people frequently ask you for help with?

Step 5: Plan Your Progression Choose ONE idea from Step 4 and outline how you'll progress through the stages:

- How could you first increase your hourly rate (Stage 2)?
- How could you systemize this to require less time (Stage 3)?
- How could you make it truly passive (Stage 4)?

Step 6: Set Your First Milestone Set a specific, measurable goal for the next 90 days:

- What will you create or launch?
- How much time will you invest?
- What's your target for first passive income dollar?

Step 7: Download Resources Visit our companion website at https ://www.FreedomDayMethod.com/book to download:

- Passive Income Idea Generator worksheet
- Treasure Hunter Assessment tool
- Stage Progression Planning template

Remember: Start with one treasure type and one idea. Master that before moving to the next. The goal isn't to do everything - it's to escape the Time Prison by creating income that doesn't require your constant presence.

Your treasure hunt starts now. Which type of treasure will you pursue first?

Chapter Fourteen

Freedom Day Method Step 6 - Achieving Your Freedom Day - 125% MRI Goal

Sometimes the worst moments in our lives lead to the most important realizations.

After that conversation with my business partner about buying me out, I spent seven days in complete emotional chaos. I was mad. I was hurt. And honestly, I was scared about what the future looked like.

I didn't know what the valuation of our firm would be. I didn't know what my cashflow from the sale would look like. And I definitely didn't know what I wanted to do when I grew up.

The uncertainty was killing me.

The Only Thing I Could Control

During those seven days before I left for the conference in Ojai, California, I felt completely powerless. My business partner was driving the valuation process. I had no control over the timeline. I couldn't predict what opportunities might be available after the sale.

But there was one thing I could control: I could look at what my MRI was.

So I did the math.

I pulled out all my spreadsheets and calculated exactly what Crystal and I needed to live on each month. Then I tried to estimate what the passive income from the business sale would generate.

When I ran the numbers, something incredible happened.

Even with my conservative estimates, I realized I was looking at around 156% of my monthly MRI from what I guessed the sale would be.

Holy crap. I had reached my Freedom Day.

What Freedom Day Really Means

Freedom Day is the moment when your passive income reaches 125% of your Minimum Required Income. Not 100%. Not 110%. 125%.

Why 125%? Because life happens.

Your car breaks down. Your roof needs repair. Your health insurance premiums go up. Inflation eats away at your purchasing power. That extra 25% isn't luxury money - it's your safety net.

Think of it this way: 100% of your MRI means you can survive. 125% means you can thrive.

More importantly, 125% gives you psychological breathing room. There's a huge difference between "barely enough" and "more than enough." That difference is the difference between financial stress and financial peace.

I Still Didn't Know What I'd Be Doing

Here's what was wild about that realization. Even though I had reached Freedom Day, I still had no idea what I wanted to do with my life.

I didn't know if I wanted to start another business. I didn't know if I wanted to travel. I didn't know if I wanted to write books or teach or consult or sit on a beach somewhere.

But here's what I did know: whatever I decided to do, it would be because I wanted to do it, not because I had to pay the bills.

That's the power of Freedom Day. It doesn't answer the question of what you should do with your life. It gives you the freedom to figure that out without financial pressure.

The Math That Changes Everything

Let me walk you through the calculation that changed my life:

Monthly Expenses (MRI): $8,000**Estimated Monthly Passive Income from Sale:** $12,500**Calculation:** $12,500 ÷ $8,000 = 156%

I was 31% above my Freedom Day target.

Now, I still had to wait for the actual sale to close. I still had to see if my estimates were accurate. But for the first time in months, I could breathe.

Whatever happened next, Crystal and I were going to be okay.

What Happens When You Hit 125%

Reaching 125% of your MRI creates a psychological shift that's hard to describe unless you've experienced it.

Suddenly, difficult conversations at work don't spike your blood pressure. You start speaking up in meetings because you're not afraid of consequences. You begin thinking about "what if" scenarios instead of "what if I lose my job" scenarios.

Most importantly, you start making decisions from abundance instead of scarcity.

When I arrived at that conference in Ojai, I wasn't the same person. I was still annoyed with the situation, I was still a bit lost, however I was calmer and confident that financially we were free.

The Three Phases of Freedom Day

Phase 1: Approaching Freedom Day (90-95% MRI) This is when you start feeling different about work. You're not quite there yet, but you can see the finish line. You start taking more risks and speaking up more because financial fear is loosening its grip.

Phase 2: Crossing the Threshold (100-125% MRI) This phase can be confusing. You might feel like you should quit your job immediately, or you might feel afraid to believe it's real. Take your time here. Let the reality sink in.

Phase 3: Living Freedom Day (125%+ MRI) This is when the psychological shift fully happens. Work becomes something you choose to do, not something you have to do. Every day becomes a conscious decision about how you want to spend your time.

How to Verify You've Reached Freedom Day

Before you make any major life decisions, you need to make sure you've actually reached Freedom Day. Here's how:

Step 1: Calculate Your True MRI Go back to Chapter 9 and update your MRI with real numbers from the past 12 months. Use actual expenses, not estimates.

Step 2: Verify Your Passive Income Make sure your passive income is truly passive and reliable. Rental income that requires constant management isn't passive. Business income that needs your daily involvement isn't passive.

Step 3: Test the 125% Threshold Your passive income should exceed your MRI by at least 25% for three consecutive months. One good month doesn't count.

Step 4: Stress Test Your Plan What if your biggest income stream disappeared tomorrow? What if your largest expense doubled? Your Freedom Day should be robust enough to handle these scenarios.

The Emotional Rollercoaster

Reaching Freedom Day isn't just a financial milestone. It's an emotional and psychological transformation that can mess with your head.

You might experience disbelief: "Is this really happening? Am I actually financially free?"

You might feel overwhelmed: "Now what? I have infinite options!"

You might have an identity crisis: "If I'm not defined by my job, who am I?"

All of this is normal. It took me about six months to fully process the psychological shift. Give yourself time to adjust.

Freedom Day Story – Andrey Kozlov

Adapting to the New World of Digital Sales

Andrey Kozlov's story, as told on the Freedom Nation Podcast, is a compelling tale of entrepreneurial success through innovation and adaptability.

With a background in digital marketing, Kozlov initially struggled with various online ventures, including T-shirt sales and managing online dating profiles. However, his breakthrough came with e-commerce and Shopify drop-shipping.

Kozlov capitalized on the emerging opportunity of Facebook Marketplace's "Buy now" button, a game-changer for his business model.

He perfected a system of finding trending items on platforms like eBay, Walmart, and Amazon and re-selling them on Facebook Marketplace at a markup without needing paid ads.

Starting in July 2020, by October, his venture had grown enough to allow him to quit his day job.

Kozlov's innovative approach to online sales and his strategic use of social media platforms demonstrate the power of e-commerce in the digital age. His story is a testament to the potential of harnessing online tools and market trends to build a successful, scalable business.

Check out my interview with Andrey at our companion website at https://www.FreedomDayMethod.com/book

Your Freedom Day Is Coming

The most beautiful thing about Freedom Day is that it's not about having enough money to never work again. It's about having enough passive income that work becomes a choice, not a necessity.

When you reach 125% of your MRI, you join a small group of people who get to wake up every morning and decide how they want to spend their day based on their values and desires, not their financial obligations.

That's worth every sacrifice you're making now to get there.

Chapter Homework: Preparing for Your Freedom Day

Objective: To create a comprehensive plan for recognizing, verifying, and transitioning into your Freedom Day.

Instructions:

Step 1: Update Your MRI Calculation Go back to Chapter 9 and recalculate your MRI using actual expenses from the past 12 months. Don't use estimates - use real numbers from your bank statements and credit card bills.

Step 2: Calculate Your Freedom Day Target Multiply your updated MRI by 1.25. This is the monthly passive income you need to achieve Freedom Day.

Step 3: Track Your Current Progress Create a simple spreadsheet with:

- Current monthly passive income by source
- Total monthly passive income
- Percentage of MRI currently covered
- Gap remaining to reach 125%

Step 4: Project Your Timeline Based on your current passive income growth rate, when do you project you'll reach Freedom Day? What would need to change to accelerate that timeline?

Step 5: Plan Your Verification Process Write down exactly how you'll verify that you've reached Freedom Day:

- How will you confirm your passive income is truly passive?
- What stress tests will you run on your income streams?
- How many consecutive months at 125% will you require before declaring Freedom Day?

Step 6: Prepare for the Emotional Journey Write down your thoughts on:

- How do you think you'll feel when you reach Freedom Day?
- What fears do you have about financial freedom?
- What will give your life meaning when work becomes optional?

Step 7: Design Your Freedom Day Celebration: How will you celebrate when you reach Freedom Day? This might seem premature, but having something to look forward to will help keep you motivated during the challenging months ahead.

Remember: Freedom Day isn't the end of your financial journey - it's the beginning of your freedom journey. The goal isn't to stop growing your wealth; it's to reach the point where growing your wealth becomes optional instead of mandatory.

Chapter Fifteen

Freedom Day Method Step 7 - To Quit or Not to Quit That Is The Question

I made a huge mistake.

Back from California and with a week of planning out what the future of my business life would look like, I immediately jumped into launching a new financial practice, this time structured around Freedom Day.

I immediately stopped doing anything to help the existing practice grow because it would not benefit me at all. I even moved into a vacant office in our coworking space to begin separating my two lives.

The problem was that the sale of the business would take another 6 months to complete.

Looking back now, this was exactly the wrong thing to do.

What I Should Have Done Instead

What I did wrong - and what I would suggest anyone reaching their Freedom Day do instead - is take some time. At least 6 months to sit back, relax, and celebrate.

Take a vacation. Pick a few bigger items off of your bucket list and do them. More importantly, investigate what you will do next. Will it be staying on with your current employer, or will you leave and pursue your passions outside?

There is no right or wrong answer.

But there is a wrong approach: making major life decisions in the immediate aftermath of reaching Freedom Day.

The Freedom Day Rush

Here's what happens when you reach Freedom Day: you get a massive rush of excitement and liberation. You want to change everything immediately. You want to quit, start something new, travel the world, or completely reinvent your life.

I felt all of that. The moment I realized I was financially free, I wanted to burn the bridges to my old life and sprint toward my new one.

That was a mistake.

Why You Need the Pause

Reaching Freedom Day is like winning the lottery, but instead of having six months to claim your prize, you have the rest of your life to decide what to do with it.

The decisions you make in the first few weeks after reaching Freedom Day will shape the next chapter of your life. Those decisions deserve more thought than I gave them.

Here's why taking 6 months to pause is crucial:

1. Your emotions are running high. You're excited, relieved, maybe even a little overwhelmed. These aren't the best conditions for making life-altering decisions.

2. You haven't fully processed the psychological shift. It takes months to really understand what financial freedom means for your identity and daily life.

3. You might burn bridges you'll regret burning. I damaged relationships by immediately disengaging from the existing practice. Some of those relationships took years to repair.

4. You need time to explore your options. There are probably opportunities you haven't even considered yet.

5. You deserve to celebrate. You just accomplished something most people never will. Take time to enjoy it.

My Rushed Decision Consequences

Because I jumped immediately into launching a new practice, I created several problems:

I was trying to build something new while still tied to something old. The business sale took 6 months to complete, so I was essentially working two jobs - managing the transition of the old practice while trying to launch the new one.

I created unnecessary stress during what should have been a celebration period. Instead of enjoying my Freedom Day achievement, I was grinding again.

I made decisions based on emotion rather than strategy. I was so eager to get away from the old business that I didn't think carefully about what I actually wanted to do next.

Most importantly, I missed the opportunity to truly explore what I wanted my life to look like.

The Six-Month Freedom Day Sabbatical

If I could do it over again, here's what I would have done:

Month 1: Celebrate and Decompress Take a real vacation. Not a working vacation, but a complete break from business thinking. Let your nervous system calm down from years of financial stress.

Month 2: Bucket List Exploration Pick 2-3 items from your bucket list and do them. Travel somewhere you've always wanted to go. Try something you've always wanted to try. Remember what it feels like to pursue experiences instead of income.

Month 3: Relationship Investment Spend quality time with family and friends. Many of these relationships probably suffered during your intense focus on reaching Freedom Day. Reconnect.

Month 4: Option Investigation Now you can start thinking about work. But don't jump into anything. Explore. Talk to people. Research industries. Consider possibilities you never could have afforded to consider before.

Month 5: Experimentation Try things on a small scale. Volunteer with organizations you're interested in. Take on consulting projects in areas that intrigue you. Test your assumptions.

Month 6: Decision Making Now, with five months of perspective and exploration, you're ready to make thoughtful decisions about what comes next.

The Decision Framework You Need

When you do reach the point of making decisions about your work future - after you've taken time to pause and explore - here are the tools that will help:

The Love vs. Hate Assessment

Before you decide whether to stay or go, get honest about your current situation.

Draw a line down the middle of a piece of paper. On the left, write "What I Love About My Current Work." On the right, "What I Hate About My Current Work."

Example - What You Might Love:

- Working with smart, ambitious people
- Solving complex problems
- Seeing results from your efforts
- The intellectual challenge
- Flexible schedule aspects
- Good compensation

Example - What You Might Hate:

- Meetings that could have been emails
- Difficult personalities you have to manage
- Administrative paperwork
- Feeling obligated to say yes to everything
- Constant pressure to be "on"

This exercise helps you separate the core work from the job structure. You might love what you do but hate how you have to do it.

The Ben Franklin Decision Method

Once you've taken time to explore and are ready to make decisions, Benjamin Franklin had a method that's incredibly helpful.

Take a sheet of paper and draw a line down the middle. On one side, write all the reasons to quit. On the other side, write all the reasons to stay.

But here's the key: Don't just count the items. Weight them by importance.

"Reasons to Quit" Might Include:

- More time for bucket list goals
- No more stressful deadlines
- Freedom to travel without work interruptions
- Ability to focus on passion projects
- Complete control over schedule

"Reasons to Stay" Might Include:

- You genuinely enjoy the core work
- The work provides intellectual stimulation
- Additional income to accelerate wealth building
- Professional relationships you value
- Structure and purpose in your days

When you weight these by importance, you often discover that your reasons aren't about money anymore - since you don't need the income. They're about fulfillment, purpose, and how you want to spend your time.

The Psychological Shift

Here's what I learned during those chaotic 6 months while the sale was completing: work feels completely different when you don't have to do it.

Before Freedom Day, difficult clients stressed me out because I needed their money. After Freedom Day, difficult clients just became people I could choose not to work with.

Before Freedom Day, saying no to projects felt risky. After Freedom Day, saying no felt empowering.

Before Freedom Day, I worried about job security. After Freedom Day, I worried about... well, nothing work-related.

The psychological shift is profound. You go from being an employee (even if you're self-employed) to being someone who chooses to contribute their talents to the world.

The Lesson I Learned

Eventually, I did launch that new financial practice focused on Freedom Day principles. But it took much longer than it should have because I was trying to do it while managing the transition of the old business.

If I had taken 6 months to pause, explore, and plan, I would have:

- Made better decisions about the structure of the new practice
- Avoided burning bridges with the old business
- Started the new venture from a position of clarity rather than reaction
- Actually enjoyed the transition instead of being stressed by it

Most importantly, I would have given myself permission to consider options I never even explored because I was so focused on immediately doing something different.

What About You?

As you approach your own Freedom Day, start thinking about what you actually want, not what you think you should want or what you think you need to do immediately.

Do you love your work but hate your boss? Maybe the answer is finding the same work with a different company - but take time to explore that option thoroughly.

Do you love your company but hate your role? Maybe the answer is switching departments or negotiating a different position - but don't rush into those conversations.

Do you love everything about your work? Maybe the answer is staying put and enjoying the psychological freedom that comes with knowing you could leave anytime.

Do you hate going to work every day? Maybe the answer is quitting the moment you hit Freedom Day - but take time to figure out what you want to do next.

There's no right answer. There's only your answer. And finding your answer takes time.

The Third Option Nobody Talks About

Most people think there are two choices after Freedom Day: keep working or quit completely.

But there's a third option that many people miss: redesign how you work.

This is where taking 6 months to explore really pays off. During that time, you can:

- Negotiate a four-day week
- Switch to project-based consulting
- Take a sabbatical and come back refreshed
- Start saying no to the parts of your job you hate and yes only to the parts you love
- Propose remote work or flexible scheduling
- Move to a different role within your company
- Become a part-time advisor instead of full-time employee

Freedom Day gives you leverage to have these conversations. Your boss knows you don't need the job, which paradoxically makes you more valuable as an employee - if you choose to remain one.

The Questions That Matter (After You've Taken Time)

Before you make any decisions about work after Freedom Day, spend your 6-month exploration period answering these questions:

1. What would I do if money wasn't a factor?This is the most important question because, after Freedom Day, money really isn't a factor anymore. But don't answer this in week one - live with the question for months.

2. What gives my life meaning and purpose?Some people find purpose in their careers. Others find it in family, hobbies, or volunteer work. You need time to figure out what really drives you when financial pressure is removed.

3. How do I want to spend my time?You have roughly 16 waking hours every day. How do you want to fill them? This might be very different from how you've been forced to fill them.

4. What would I regret not trying?Freedom Day gives you permission to take risks you couldn't take before. But which risks are calling to you? This takes exploration to discover.

5. What kind of legacy do I want to leave?This isn't just about money. It's about impact, contribution, and how you want to be remembered. These insights develop over time, not in a moment of decision.

Freedom Day Story – Robert Poole

Deciding to Fire Yourself

Robert Poole's story is a compelling tale of transformation from a military officer to a successful entrepreneur. Poole's journey began at West Point, leading to a career as an army officer.

He ventured into various sales roles post-military, eventually joining Merrill Lynch in the late 90s. His entrepreneurial spirit led him to start a website design firm, which pivoted to a B2B appointment setting and lead generation firm, achieving multi-million-dollar success.

Tragedy struck in 2017 when Poole's business partner unexpectedly passed away, leaving Poole to manage the entire operation. This experience made Poole realize he was more of an operator than an owner, prompting him to transform his role in the business.

He focused on creating systems and processes to ensure the business could thrive without his constant involvement. Poole's journey illustrates the challenges and rewards of entrepreneurship and the importance of adaptability and strategic thinking in business.

Robert has consulted with other business owners and helped them replicate his success at changing their businesses from operator-based to owner-based.

You can watch my full interview with Robert on our companion website, www.RetirementTrapBook.com/videos.

Testing Your Decision

Whatever you decide about work after Freedom Day - and after you've taken proper time to explore - test it first.

If you're thinking about quitting, try taking a long vacation first. How do you feel after two weeks of not working? Relaxed and recharged, or bored and restless?

If you're thinking about staying, try renegotiating your terms. Ask for more flexibility, better projects, or a different role. See how it feels to work from a position of strength instead of need.

If you're thinking about starting something new, try it as a side project first. You have the luxury of experimenting without risking your livelihood.

The Beauty of Optionality

Here's the most beautiful thing about reaching Freedom Day: you're not making a permanent decision.

If you quit your job and realize you miss it, you can find another job. If you stay and realize you hate it, you can quit. If you try something new and it doesn't work out, you can try something else.

Freedom Day gives you optionality. You get to experiment with your life in ways that most people can't afford to.

But this experimentation works best when you're thoughtful about it, not reactive.

My Life After Learning This Lesson

Three years after that rushed decision to immediately launch a new practice, I finally created the work life I actually wanted.

I work with clients I love on projects that challenge me. I say no to everything that doesn't excite me. I take month-long vacations without checking email. I write books, start podcasts, and pursue passion projects.

Most importantly, I never feel trapped again.

But it took me longer to get there because I didn't take the time to pause and explore my options thoughtfully. I was so eager to escape my old situation that I jumped into a new one without really considering what I wanted that new situation to look like.

Don't make my mistake. When you reach Freedom Day, celebrate it. Take time to explore. Figure out what you actually want before you make decisions about what comes next.

Work can become something you choose to do, not something you have to do. But choosing well requires time and thoughtfulness.

Chapter Homework: Planning Your Post-Freedom Day Transition

Objective: To create a thoughtful 6-month exploration plan for after you reach Freedom Day, avoiding the mistake of making rushed decisions about your work future.

Instructions:

Step 1: Design Your Freedom Day Sabbatical Plan your 6-month exploration period:

- Month 1 (Celebrate & Decompress): What vacation or break will you take?
- Month 2 (Bucket List): Which 2-3 bucket list items will you pursue?
- Month 3 (Relationships): Which relationships need attention and investment?

- Month 4 (Investigation): What work options will you explore?
- Month 5 (Experimentation): How will you test different possibilities?
- Month 6 (Decision): What framework will you use to decide?

Step 2: Create Your Work Assessment (For Later) Prepare the tools you'll use during Month 4:

- Love vs. Hate assessment template for your current work
- Ben Franklin method setup (reasons to quit vs. stay, with importance ratings)
- List of people you'll talk to during your investigation phase

Step 3: Identify Your Big Questions Write down these questions to live with during your exploration:

- What would I do if money wasn't a factor?
- What gives my life meaning and purpose?
- How do I want to spend my time?
- What would I regret not trying?
- What kind of legacy do I want to leave?

Step 4: Plan Your Option Exploration List the work possibilities you want to investigate:

- Staying with current employer with modifications
- Finding similar work with different company
- Starting your own business or consulting practice
- Pursuing completely different career

- Taking extended break from work
- Combining work with passion projects

Step 5: Design Your Testing Strategy For each option you want to explore, plan how you'll test it:

- Conversations you'll have
- Experiences you'll try
- Small experiments you'll run
- Timeline for each test

Step 6: Set Your Boundaries Commit to avoiding rushed decisions:

- What decisions will you NOT make in your first month after Freedom Day?
- How will you handle pressure from others to make quick decisions?
- What will you say to people asking "What's next?" before you're ready to answer?

Step 7: Create Your Support System Identify who will help you during this transition:

- Who can you talk through options with?
- Who will hold you accountable to taking time before deciding?
- Who has experience with similar transitions?

Remember: The biggest mistake you can make after reaching Freedom Day is rushing into major life decisions while your emotions are high and you haven't had time to fully process this new reality. Give yourself the gift of time. You've worked hard to earn this freedom - use it thoughtfully.

Chapter Sixteen

Freedom Day Method Step 8 - Embracing the Freedom Day Lifestyle

The business sale was finally finishing up at the end of 2022.

After months of legal paperwork, due diligence, and transition planning, I knew I would have a lump sum of money as part of the sale. So Crystal and I sat down to prioritize what we would do at that point.

The easy decisions were obvious: pay off some debt, put money into reserves for savings, invest some money in real estate to generate extra income.

But most importantly, it was time to treat Crystal and me to a vacation.

Instead of the usual vacation, we decided to combine this first post-Freedom Day trip with our bucket lists. Each of us had completed our own bucket lists with some common things we wanted to do and others that each of us wanted separately.

Our first trip was a week in London.

Living the Dream

That London trip was everything I'd imagined Freedom Day would feel like - and some things I hadn't expected.

We were there for Valentine's Day, which was one of my bucket list goals. We had awesome lunches at three restaurants we'd seen on the Food Network - something both of us had wanted to do. Crystal got her high tea at Kensington Gardens. I got to drive an Aston Martin at Silverstone Raceway, which actually knocked two bucket list items off my list at once.

We visited the Harry Potter experience together, something both of us had been excited about. We watched Wicked in the West End with the full VIP experience - another shared bucket list item.

But here's what struck me most about that trip: we weren't checking our phones constantly to see if we could afford things. We weren't calculating whether we should skip the VIP experience to save money. We weren't stressed about missing work.

For the first time in our adult lives, we were truly present for our own vacation.

The Reality of Living Freedom Day

That London trip taught me something important about what Freedom Day actually means in daily life. It's not just about having enough money to quit your job - though that's part of it. It's about living without the constant background anxiety about money that most people carry every day.

When you're truly living your Freedom Day, you make decisions differently:

You choose restaurants based on what sounds good, not what you can afford.

You book the hotel room you actually want, not the cheapest one available.

You don't skip experiences because of cost - you skip them because you're not interested.

You tip generously without thinking twice about it.

You're never stressed about unexpected expenses.

Most importantly, you spend time thinking about what you want to do with your life instead of what you have to do to pay bills.

The Four Pillars of Living Freedom Day

Over the past few years of living in Freedom Day, I've learned that maintaining this lifestyle requires attention to four key areas:

Pillar 1: Protecting Your Base

Your Freedom Day calculation assumes your passive income will continue. That means you need to protect and maintain the systems that generate that income.

If you have rental properties, maintain them properly. If you have investments, rebalance them periodically. If you have business income, keep the systems running smoothly.

Freedom Day isn't set-it-and-forget-it. It's set-it-and-maintain-it.

We check our rental properties quarterly, review our investment portfolio every six months, and assess our overall financial position annually. Not because we're worried, but because we want to stay free.

Pillar 2: Strategic Growth and Business Optimization

Just because you've reached Freedom Day doesn't mean you should stop building wealth. But now you can be strategic instead of desperate.

Since reaching Freedom Day, we've continued to invest and build our real estate portfolio. I've developed some new strategies around our investment portfolio that now generate a significant amount of cash flow each month - income that goes directly into our freedom fund.

More importantly, I made some tough business decisions that I couldn't have made when I was dependent on every dollar of income. We closed two non-performing businesses and sold another one. Instead of trying to keep everything alive out of financial fear, I consolidated the remaining businesses into three focused lines of business.

Now I spend my time improving profitability and cash flow in each of those three areas instead of spreading myself thin across six different ventures. The result? Each business performs better, requires less of my time, and generates more reliable income.

This is what strategic growth looks like after Freedom Day. You're not scrambling to create income from every possible source. You're optimizing the sources that actually work and eliminating the ones that don't.

Before Freedom Day, I was afraid to close or sell underperforming businesses because I needed every dollar they generated, even if they were barely profitable. After Freedom Day, I could make decisions based on long-term strategy instead of short-term cash flow needs.

Pillar 3: Intentional Spending

One of the biggest mistakes people make after reaching financial freedom is lifestyle inflation. You start spending more simply because you can, not because it adds value to your life.

That London trip was intentional spending. Every dollar we spent was aligned with our bucket list goals and our values.

But it would be easy to let that turn into always flying first class, always staying at the most expensive hotels, always ordering the most expensive wine. Not because we particularly want those things, but because we can afford them.

Freedom Day gives you permission to spend money on what matters to you. It doesn't give you permission to spend money carelessly.

Pillar 4: Purpose and Meaning

This is the one that surprised me the most. When you don't have to work for money, you have to figure out why you're working at all.

Some people find this liberating. Others find it terrifying.

Without the external motivation of needing to pay bills, you have to find internal motivation for how you spend your time. This can lead to an identity crisis if you've defined yourself by your job for most of your adult life.

For me, it took about a year to figure out what I wanted to do with my time. Writing this book, creating the Freedom Day Method program, helping other people achieve financial freedom - these became my new purposes.

But that purpose had to come from within, not from external financial pressure.

The Bucket List Revolution

That London trip also taught us something about how to approach our bucket lists after Freedom Day.

Before, our bucket lists were dreams - things we hoped to do someday if we ever had enough money and time.

After Freedom Day, our bucket lists became project plans.

We now approach bucket list items systematically. We plan 2-3 major bucket list experiences per year, research them thoroughly, and execute them properly. We're not rushing through them because we're afraid the money will run out.

This year, we're planning a month in Italy, focusing on cooking classes in Tuscany and art museums in Florence. Next year, we're looking at a safari in Kenya and a food tour through Japan.

The difference is that these aren't dreams anymore. They're scheduled events.

Avoiding the Freedom Day Traps

Living in Freedom Day isn't all bucket list vacations and stress-free decisions. There are some traps you need to avoid:

The Guilt Trap: Feeling guilty about spending money or not working, even though you've earned the right to both.

The Boredom Trap: Having too much free time without enough purpose, leading to depression or restlessness.

The Inflation Trap: Letting your lifestyle expand beyond what your Freedom Day income can sustain.

The Complacency Trap: Assuming your Freedom Day will last forever without maintaining the systems that created it.

The Isolation Trap: Losing connection with friends who are still in the daily grind of working for money.

The key to avoiding these traps is staying intentional about how you live your Freedom Day, not just drifting through it.

You Don't Have to Wait to Start Living

Here's one of the most important things I've learned about the Freedom Day journey: you can start living the Freedom Day lifestyle long before you reach full financial freedom.

Use your bucket list as a reward system along the way as you build up passive income streams. Look for ways to check off some bucket list items while you're still working toward your Freedom Day goal.

In 2023, what began with my driving an Aston Martin at Silverstone turned into 12 similar experiences that I called "Jeff's Planes, Trains, and Automobiles Adventure." These were funded by a specific Freedom Engine that I had created - a real estate investment - specifically for that purpose.

Each month for 12 months, I did one experience that could be had for less than $500. I drove a Lamborghini at the COTA track in Austin. I flew on a WW2 bomber. I rode in a cigarette boat in Miami, feeling like I was in an episode of Miami Vice. I rode on the world's largest remaining steam engine. And many other similar experiences.

The key was creating a dedicated income stream - what I call a Freedom Engine - specifically to fund these adventures. Instead of waiting until I had total financial freedom to start enjoying life, I built one small piece of passive income specifically to fund bucket list experiences.

This approach does two powerful things:

First, it gives you immediate rewards during the long journey toward Freedom Day. Instead of grinding for years with no fun, you get monthly reminders of why you're working so hard.

Second, it proves to you that the system works. Every time you fund a bucket list experience with passive income, you're experiencing in miniature what full Freedom Day will feel like.

You don't need $12,500 per month in passive income to start living aspects of the Freedom Day lifestyle. You just need enough passive income to fund one bucket list experience per month, or per quarter, or even per year.

Start small. Build one Freedom Engine. Use it to fund one meaningful experience. Then build another one.

Freedom Day Story – Marilyn Nichols

Starting Over on Your Terms
Marilyn Nichols never planned to retire in the traditional sense. For years, she ran Happy Puppy Tutoring, a mobile dog training and boarding business that became one of the most trusted in her area. She built it from scratch after walking away from corporate life, leaning into her love for animals—and her uncanny ability to understand them. But after years of working long hours, juggling dozens of dogs, and running a business largely on her own, she started to think about what came next.

Three years before her retirement, we started having conversations about what life could look like beyond the business. Marilyn didn't want to slow down—she wanted to redirect her energy. When her Freedom Day arrived, she sold the business and moved to the country with her partner, Mike. That's where her second act began. Today, Marilyn writes science fiction novels, sculpts in her art studio, and takes weekly voice lessons—all part of a daily rhythm that feels more like purpose than retirement.

In our interview, she shares the lessons she's learned about planning ahead, creating a life you actually want to wake up to, and embracing who you are at every stage of the journey. Her story is proof that Freedom Day isn't about quitting. It's about *starting over on your terms.*

Watch Marilyn's full story at: www.freedomdaymethod.com/videos

What Living Freedom Day Really Means

Two years into living my Freedom Day, here's what I've learned:

Freedom Day isn't about never working again. It's about working because you choose to, not because you have to.

Freedom Day isn't about spending money on everything you want. It's about having the security to spend money on what truly matters to you.

Freedom Day isn't about having no financial stress. It's about having the kind of financial stress that comes from abundance instead of scarcity.

Freedom Day isn't about being happy all the time. It's about having the space to figure out what actually makes you happy.

Most importantly, Freedom Day isn't the end of your journey. It's the beginning of a completely different kind of life - one where you get to decide how to spend your time based on your values instead of your financial obligations.

Your Freedom Day Awaits

The eight steps of the Freedom Day Method aren't just about reaching a financial milestone. They're about creating a life where money serves you instead of you serving money.

That London trip with Crystal wasn't just a vacation. It was proof that the system works. It was evidence that all the sacrifice, planning, and discipline along the way was worth it.

Every time you choose the generic brand to save money, remember that London trip is waiting for you.

Every time you say no to an expensive dinner out, remember that your bucket list is waiting for you.

Every time you invest money instead of spending it, remember that freedom is waiting for you.

The Freedom Day Method works. But only if you work it.

Your Freedom Day is coming. And when it arrives, you'll be ready to live it.

Chapter Homework: Designing Your Freedom Day Life

Objective: To create a comprehensive plan for living your Freedom Day once you achieve it, including bucket list execution, wealth maintenance, and lifestyle design.

Instructions:

Step 1: Create Your Bucket List Strategy Develop your post-Freedom Day bucket list approach:

- List your top 20 bucket list items
- Separate individual vs. shared goals (if you have a partner)
- Estimate time and cost for each item
- Prioritize your top 5 for the first two years after Freedom Day
- Create a timeline for bucket list execution

Step 2: Design Your Wealth Maintenance Plan Plan how you'll protect your Freedom Day:

- How often will you review your passive income streams?
- What maintenance will your income sources require?
- How will you handle potential income disruptions?
- What's your plan for continuing to grow wealth after Freedom Day?
- Who will help you manage your investments and properties?

Step 3: Set Your Intentional Spending Guidelines Create rules to avoid lifestyle inflation:

- What categories will you increase spending in after Freedom

Day?

- What categories will you keep at current levels?
- How will you decide if a purchase aligns with your values?
- What's your system for avoiding impulse purchases?
- How much will you allocate to bucket list vs. daily living?

Step 4: Plan Your Purpose and Meaning Prepare for the psychological transition:

- What will give your life meaning when work becomes optional?
- What activities or causes are you passionate about?
- How will you structure your days without external work requirements?
- What new skills or interests do you want to pursue?
- How will you stay connected to community and relationships?

Step 5: Identify Your Freedom Day Traps Plan to avoid common pitfalls:

- How will you handle guilt about your financial freedom?
- What will you do if you feel bored or restless?
- How will you resist lifestyle inflation pressure?
- What systems will keep you from becoming complacent?
- How will you maintain relationships with people still working?

Step 6: Design Your Annual Freedom Day Review Create a system for staying on track:

- Annual financial review process and timeline
- Bucket list progress assessment
- Lifestyle and spending evaluation
- Purpose and meaning check-in
- Adjustments needed for the following year

Step 7: Plan Your Freedom Day Celebration Design how you'll mark this milestone:

- How will you celebrate reaching Freedom Day?
- What will your first post-Freedom Day trip include?
- Who will you share this achievement with?
- What traditions will you start to commemorate this milestone?
- How will you document and remember this moment?

Remember: Freedom Day isn't a finish line - it's a starting line for a completely different kind of life. The planning you do now for how you'll live your Freedom Day will determine whether you truly enjoy your financial freedom or drift through it without purpose. Make your Freedom Day intentional, meaningful, and aligned with your deepest values.

Chapter Seventeen

Now Is the Time - Launching Your Journey to Freedom Day

As I finish writing this book today in June of 2025, almost 3 years after my Freedom Day, I live a life completely different from what I thought it would be.

Although I have continued to build my new financial practice, it hasn't been the big deal that I thought it would be. I have grown it slower, choosing people that I wanted to work with instead of people I had to work with.

I began to write again after almost 10 years. Including this book, I have written over 14 non-fiction books and have recently begun writing a series of fiction books - which is what I have dreamed of doing since I left college.

I share my advice to the world on 3 podcasts. I have 3 businesses with over 17 different income streams.

More than anything, I can stop at any time. I can work as much or as little as I want, and take off and travel whenever we want.

Over the next 18 months, Crystal and I are working hard to adapt our businesses to be able to run them from anywhere in the world and live one of our biggest bucket list items: living for 3 months in the English countryside.

This is what Freedom Day actually looks like. Not what I expected, but exactly what I needed.

The Reality of Your Freedom Day

Here's what I've learned about Freedom Day after living it for three years: it's not about the life you plan to live. It's about having the freedom to live whatever life emerges from your authentic interests and values.

Before Freedom Day, I thought I knew exactly what I wanted to do. Build a big financial practice. Help lots of people. Make lots of money.

After Freedom Day, I discovered what I actually wanted to do. Write fiction. Choose my clients carefully. Help people through books and podcasts instead of just one-on-one meetings. Build businesses that can run from anywhere in the world.

The difference isn't about the specific activities. The difference is about the motivation behind them.

Before Freedom Day, I was building businesses because I had to generate income. After Freedom Day, I'm building businesses because I want to create value.

Before Freedom Day, I was working with clients who could pay my fees. After Freedom Day, I'm working with clients whose lives I genuinely want to improve.

Before Freedom Day, I had no time to write books. After Freedom Day, I am enjoying the ability to share my writing with the world.

This is the real promise of Freedom Day: not that you'll do what you planned, but that you'll be free to do what matters.

Your Freedom Day Blueprint: The Complete System

Throughout this book, you've been building your Freedom Day Blueprint step by step. Now it's time to put all the pieces together.

Your complete Freedom Day Method follows these 8 steps:

Step 1: Calculating Your MRI - The Key to Financial Clarity-Determine your Minimum Required Income - the monthly amount you need to maintain your desired lifestyle without working.

Step 2: Creating Your Bucket List Define what you want to do with your freedom and create meaningful goals that will motivate you throughout your journey.

Step 3: Retraining Your Brain for Financial Success Develop the mindset and habits necessary to build wealth and make decisions that support your Freedom Day goals.

Step 4: Kill Your Debt with The Debt Snowball Method Eliminate debt systematically to reduce your MRI and free up more money for wealth building.

Step 5: Transitioning to Passive Income – The Game Changer Build income streams that generate money without requiring your daily time and attention.

Step 6: Achieving Your Freedom Day - 125% MRI Goal Reach 125% of your MRI in passive income - your official Freedom Day milestone.

Step 7: To Quit or Not to Quit That Is The Question Decide whether to leave your job immediately or transition gradually from earned to passive income.

Step 8: Embracing the Freedom Day Lifestyle Live your new life of financial freedom while maintaining and growing your wealth.

Each step builds on the previous ones. Each step gets you closer to the life you want to live.

The Stories That Prove It Works

Throughout this book, you've met people at different stages of their Freedom Day journey:

Scott Danner left his corporate job to build a business around his passion for helping companies with safety and compliance. His Freedom Day gave him the security to pursue work that matters to him.

Robert Chen achieved his Freedom Day through real estate investing while continuing to work in tech. His passive income gave him the confidence to make strategic career moves without financial pressure.

Marilyn Nichols sold her dog training business and moved to the country to write science fiction novels and pursue art. Her Freedom Day gave her permission to explore creative interests she'd always loved.

Vicki Noethling transitioned from 40 years in corporate environments to become a speaker, trainer, and podcast host. Her Freedom Day gave her the foundation to build a second career around helping others develop leadership skills.

These aren't exceptional people with unusual advantages. They're ordinary people who followed the Freedom Day Method and created extraordinary lives.

The only difference between them and you is that they started.

Freedom Day Story – Vicki Noethling

The Second Act is Even Better

Vicki Noethling's story showcases her transformative journey from a seasoned corporate professional to an influential speaker, trainer, and podcast host. With over 40 years in corporate environments, including roles at an accounting firm, a fast-food chain's corporate office, and a large transportation company.

Vicki retired to pivot her life towards making a difference. Her experiences led her to launch a speaker, trainer, and coaching business, followed by her podcast, "Find Your Leadership Confidence." Vicki's mission is to help others excel in communication and leadership, utilizing her vast experience to guide entrepreneurs out of isolation and toward solving their problems.

She emphasizes the power of connection, authFentic communication, and the importance of understanding one's audience, whether speaking in person or virtually. Vicki's journey is a testament to the impact of lifelong learning, adaptability, and the drive to empower others through improved communication and leadership skills.

Check out our interview with Vicki on our companion site, www.TheRetirementTrapBook.com/videos.

The Choice That Changes Everything

Right now, you have a choice to make.

You can close this book, put it on the shelf, and continue living the way you've always lived. You can keep working at a job that pays the bills but doesn't fulfill you. You can keep putting off your dreams until "someday" when you have more time, more money, more security.

Or you can start building your Freedom Day.

You can calculate your MRI this week. You can identify one expense to cut this month. You can start one side hustle in the next 90 days. You can make one real estate investment in the next year.

The Freedom Day Method works. But only if you work it.

Every person whose story appears in this book made the same choice you're facing right now. They decided to stop hoping things would get better and start making them better.

They didn't have special advantages. They didn't have perfect timing. They didn't have unlimited resources.

They had something more powerful than any of those things: they had a plan and the willingness to execute it.

Your Freedom Day Is Waiting

Three years ago, I was working 60-hour weeks, stressed about money, and dreaming of a different life.

Today, I'm writing fiction in my home office, planning a 3-month stay in the English countryside, and building businesses that can run from anywhere in the world.

The only difference between three years ago and today is that I started following the Freedom Day Method.

Your Freedom Day is waiting for you.

It's waiting for you to calculate your MRI. It's waiting for you to cut your expenses. It's waiting for you to build your first income stream. It's waiting for you to take the first step, then the second, then the third.

It's waiting for you to stop planning and start building.

The best time to start was 10 years ago. The second best time is today.

Your Freedom Day journey begins right now.

Chapter Homework: Your Freedom Day Action Plan

Objective: Create a comprehensive 90-day action plan to begin your Freedom Day journey and establish momentum for long-term success.

Step 1: Complete Your Freedom Day Vision

Write a detailed description of your Freedom Day life:

- What does a typical day look like after Freedom Day?
- Where are you living? What type of home?
- What meaningful work are you doing (if any)?
- How are you spending your time?
- What bucket list items have you accomplished?
- Who are you spending time with?
- What does "success" mean to you in this new life?

Step 2: Calculate Your Starting Point

Determine exactly where you are financially right now:

- Calculate your current MRI using the worksheet from Chapter 9
- List all current income sources and amounts
- List all current expenses and identify which are essential
- Calculate your current savings rate

- Identify your total current assets and debts
- Determine how much passive income you currently generate (if any)

Step 3: Create Your 90-Day Quick Wins Plan

Choose specific actions you can complete in the next 90 days:

- One major expense you will eliminate or reduce this month
- One income-increasing action you will take (ask for raise, find better job, start side hustle)
- One debt you will pay off or significantly reduce
- One passive income stream you will research and potentially start
- One skill you will develop that could increase your earning potential

Step 4: Design Your One-Year Freedom Day Milestones

Set specific targets for 12 months from now:

- Target MRI reduction (what will you cut it to?)
- Target income increase (earned and/or passive)
- Target debt reduction or elimination
- Target asset accumulation (savings, investments, real estate)
- Target passive income generation amount
- First major bucket list item you will fund and complete

Step 5: Build Your Support System

Identify who will help you succeed:

- Who in your life supports your Freedom Day goals?
- Who might sabotage or discourage your efforts?
- What professional help might you need (financial advisor, tax professional, real estate agent)?
- What books, courses, or resources will you use to continue learning?
- How will you track your progress and stay accountable?

Step 6: Prepare for Obstacles

Plan how you'll handle challenges:

- What expenses might increase that you haven't planned for?
- What income disruptions are possible in your situation?
- What family or social pressures might interfere with your plan?
- What personal habits or mindsets might sabotage your progress?
- How will you handle setbacks and keep moving forward?

Step 7: Schedule Your Freedom Day Review System

Create ongoing accountability:

- Weekly review: What did you accomplish this week toward Freedom Day?

- Monthly review: Are you on track with your 90-day plan?
- Quarterly review: Do you need to adjust your one-year milestones?
- Annual review: How much closer are you to your Freedom Day?
- Celebration plan: How will you reward yourself for achieving milestones?

Remember: The Freedom Day Method is not a get-rich-quick scheme. It's a systematic approach to building the life you want over time. Your willingness to start, stay consistent, and adapt when necessary will determine your success. Every action you take brings you closer to the freedom you desire.

Take the first step today. Your Freedom Day is waiting.

About The Author

Jeff Kikel

Hi, I'm Jeff Kikel.

I've spent more than 30 years helping people prepare for retirement—but not the kind you see in stock photos with sailboats and sunsets. I'm talking about real retirement. The kind where you stop working because you *want to*, not because you *have to*. The kind where you wake up with purpose, freedom, and maybe even a few bucket list items to cross off.

I'm the founder of Freedom Day Wealth Management, where we specialize in helping business owners, professionals, and families create real-world retirement income strategies. No fluff. No Wall Street double-speak. Just clear plans that work.

Alongside my wife Crystal, I've written several books on retirement, Social Security, and financial planning. We're also passionate entrepreneurs, podcasters, and lifelong learners. When we're not working with clients or writing, you'll probably find us road-tripping, cooking something we saw on the Food Network, or crossing off another bucket list goal. (Yes, I *did* drive an Aston Martin at Silverstone.)

This book was born from the stories I've lived, the people I've helped, and the lessons I've learned the hard way. If it helped you start thinking differently about your own future, then it did its job.

You can find more tools, resources, and stories like the ones in this book at:
www.FreedomDayMethod.com

Let's build your Freedom Day—together.

Keeping the Game Alive

Now that you've got the tools to take control of your retirement—and maybe even start planning your own Freedom Day—it's time to pass that knowledge on.

By leaving a quick, honest review of this book on Amazon, you can help someone else who's still stuck. Someone searching for answers. Someone who's worked hard their whole life but isn't sure how to make work optional.

Most people don't know where to turn when it comes to planning their next chapter. Your review could be the signpost they've been waiting for.

This book was written for everyday folks—small business owners, corporate warriors, families juggling real-life stuff—who want a retirement that works in the real world. If it helped you, your review can help them.

Thank you for being part of this movement. The idea of **retiring with purpose and freedom** only stays alive when we pass it on—and your review helps me do just that.

Leave your review at:

https://www.amazon.com/review/review-your-purchases/?asin
=B0FD5DMQ54

Let's help the next person get started.

– Jeff

Other Books By Jeff Kikel

Before□The□Night□Falls

A gripping crime thriller introducing Detective Marcus Vale as he navigates corruption in Brooklyn—a captivating start to the *Night Files* series .

Memory Mastery for Entrepreneurs

Boost your focus, sharpen your recall, and juggle your business with confidence. Part of the *Entrepreneur Superpowers* series.

The Business Owner's Retirement Blueprint

A clear, no-fluff guide to selling your business and planning a retirement that truly works. Book□1 in the *Exit Rich...Retire Free* series.

10 Critical Mistakes in Retirement Planning (and How to Fix Them)

Spot and avoid the most common retirement pitfalls before they derail your dreams. Book□1 in the *Stress-Free Retirement* series.

The Retirement Income Equation

Discover flexible, secure income strategies that let you retire on your terms. Book□2 in the *Stress-Free Retirement* series.

Social Security Essentials

Demystify Social Security—learn when to file and how to maximize your benefits with easy-to-follow guidance. Book□3 in the *Stress-Free Retirement* series .

Medicare Essentials

Navigate Medicare like a pro—avoid costly mistakes and get the right coverage for your needs. Book□4 in the *Stress-Free Retirement* series.

Long Term Care Essentials

Plan for aging smartly—protect yourself and your loved ones from unexpected care costs. Book□5 in the *Stress-Free Retirement* series.

Estate Planning Essentials

Preserve your legacy—keep your estate safe, avoid probate, and care for your loved ones. Book□6 in the *Stress-Free Retirement* series.

Identity Theft: The Road To Recovery

Stay one step ahead of scammers—protect your identity and recover fast if it's stolen. Book□7 in the *Stress-Free Retirement* series.

The Family Finance Playbook

Teach your family financial literacy together—build lasting wealth through simple, practical steps. Book□1 in the *Family Playbook* series.

Go to www.JeffKikel.com for updates on books, and our weekly magazine with a new mystery story per week.

www.ingramcontent.com/pod-product-compliance
Lightning Source LLC
LaVergne TN
LVHW022040200926
848481LV00003B/727

* 9 7 9 8 3 4 9 4 4 3 1 3 8 *